THE AUTHORITY OF SUNNAH

Justice Muhammad Taqi Usmani

KITAB BHAVAN
New Delhi-110002

The Authority of Sunnah

KITAB BHAVAN
Publishers, Distributors, Exporters & Importers
1784, Kalan Mahal, Darya Ganj,
New Delhi - 1100 02 (India)

Phones : (91-11) 23277392/93, 23274686, 32906494
Fax : (91-11) 23263383

Website : www.kitabbavan.net
: www.kitabbavan.com

Email : nasri@vsnl.com
: nusrat@bol.net.in

6th Edition : 2015

ISBN : 81-7151-132-5
Book Code No. : A00269

Printed & Published in India by :
Nusrat Ali Nasri for KITAB BHAVAN
1784, Kalan Mahal, Darya Ganj,
New Delhi - 1100 02 [India]

CONTENTS

بسم الله الرحمن الرحيم

الحمد لله وكفى وسلام على عباده الذين اصطفى

FOREWORD

In October 1989, I was invited to present a paper on the "Authority of the Sunnah" in an international conference held in Chicago by an international Islamic organisation.

Since long, I felt the need of a brief English booklet containing basic information on "The Sunnah of the Holy Prophet ﷺ", it's general features, the nature of it's authority and the standard of it's authenticity.

I took the opportunity to fulfil this need and wrote on the subject in a little more detail than was required in a conference of this type.

The present work is the result of the above endeavour.

This book is meant for the general reader who wants to know what the "Sunnah of the Holy Prophet ﷺ" is, how does it have a binding authority over all the Muslims for all times to come, what status has the Holy Quran given to it and what measures has the *Ummah* adopted to preserve it for the coming generations.

I hope that this humble effort will provide brief, yet clear, answers to questions of similar nature and will help understanding the true status of the 'Sunnah' as a source of Islamic Law and as a source of guidance for all Muslims in their practical lives. It will also assist, I hope, in removing certain doubts inculcated by few contemporary writers in respect of the authority of the Sunnah.

May Almighty Allah approve of this humble effort, adorne it with His pleasure and make it beneficial to the readers.

Muhammad Taqi Usmani

CHAPTER 1

SUNNAH: THE SECOND SOURCE OF ISLAMIC LAW

The *Sunnah* of the Holy Prophet Muhammad ﷺ has been accepted as an important source of Islamic law, next in importance only to the Holy Quran. This status of the *sunnah* has remained unchallenged and undisputed throughout the centuries. There have been many differences among Muslims in their juristic opinions, but the authority of the Holy Quran and the *sunnah* of the Holy Prophet was never denied by any jurist. Leaving aside some scattered individuals who separated themselves from the main stream of the Muslim population, nobody has ever refused to accept the *sunnah* of the Holy Prophet as a sacred source of the Islamic law.

The position is still the same, but some non-Muslim orientalists and some of their followers have tried, during the last century to cast some doubts in the authority or the veracity of *Hadith* and to develop a suspicious attitude towards the *Sunnah*. That is why some Muslims who are unable to study Islam through its original sources, when they read such books, often become a bit skeptical in the subject.

The present article intends, therefore, to provide an objective and simple account of the *SUNNAH* based on the original sources of Islamic learning. The purpose is not to indulge in a hot atmosphere of argumentation which has no bounds or limits, but to narrate the truth as it stands.

DEFINITION OF *SUNNAH*

The *Sunnah* has been defined by the scholars of the science of ' Hadith ' as follows:

> "A word spoken or an act done or a confirmation given by the Holy Prophet Muhammad ﷺ ."

'Confirmation' in this definition is termed in Arabic as *Taqrir*. What is meant by this term is like somebody said something, or acted in a particular manner, and his saying or act came to the knowledge of the Holy Prophet ﷺ ,and he either confirmed it in express words or remained silent without giving any indication of disapproval. Such silence, being an implied approval of the Holy Prophet ﷺ is also included in the term 'Sunnah'.

As the *Sunnah*, with all its three kinds (saying, act and confirmation), relates to the Holy Prophet ﷺ, its true status in the Islamic law cannot be ascertained without ascertaining the status of The Holy Prophet ﷺ himself.

The status of the Holy Prophet

So , the first pertinent question in the subject is: What status does a prophet occupy when he is sent to the people? Has he no higher a status than that of a message - carrier or a postman who, after delivering the letter, has no concern with it whatsoever? The answer is certainly in the negative. The prophets are not sent merely to deliver the word of Allah. They are also requried to explain the divine Book, to interpret it, to expound it, to demonstrate the ways of its application and to present a practical example of its contents. Their duty is not restricted to reciting the words of the Book, rather they are supposed to teach it and to train people to run their lives in accordance with its requirements. The Holy Quran leaves no doubt concerning this point by saying:

لَقَدْ مَنَّ اللهُ عَلَى الْمُؤْمِنِيْنَ إِذْ بَعَثَ فِيْهِمْ رَسُوْلاً
مِنْ أَنْفُسِهِمْ يَتْلُوْا عَلَيْهِمْ آيَاتِهِ وَيُزَكِّيْهِمْ وَيُعَلِّمُهُمْ
الْكِتَابَ وَالْحِكْمَةَ وَإِنْ كَانُوْا مِنْ قَبْلُ لَفِيْ ضَلاَلٍ
مُبِيْنٍ.

Allah has surely blessed the believers with His favour when He raised in their midst a Messenger from among themselves, who recites to them His verses and makes them pure and teaches them the Book and the wisdom, while they were, earlier, in an open error (3:164).

هُوَالَّذِىْ بَعَثَ فِي الأُمِّيِّيْنَ رَسُوْلاً مِنْهُمْ يَتْلُوْ
عَلَيْهِمْ آيَاتِهِ وَيُزَكِّيْهِمْ وَيُعَلِّمُهُمُ الْكِتَابَ وَالْحِكْمَةَ

He (Allah) is the One who raised up, among the unlettered, a Messenger from among themselves who recites the verses of Allah, and makes them pure and teaches them the Book and the wisdom. (62:2)

The same functions were attributed to the Holy Prophet ﷺ in the prayer of Sayyidna Ibrahim عليه السلام when, according to the Holy Quran, he prayed:

رَبَّنَا وَابْعَثْ فِيهِمْ رَسُولاً مِنْهُمْ يَتْلُو عَلَيْهِمْ
آيَاتِكَ وَيُعَلِّمُهُمُ الْكِتَابَ وَالْحِكْمَةَ وَيُزَكِّيهِمْ

Our Lord, raise in their midst a messenger from among themselves who recites to them Your verses and teaches them the Book and the wisdom and purifies them. (2: 129)

These are the terms of reference given to the Holy Prophet ﷺ which include four distinct functions and the Holy Prophet ﷺ has been entrusted with all of them:

(1) Recitation of the Verses of Allah.

(2) Teaching the Book of Allah.

(3) Teaching the Wisdom.

(4) Making the people pure.

Thus the Holy Quran leaves no ambiguities in the fact that the Holy Prophet ﷺ is not supposed to merely recite the verses and then leave it to the people to interpret and apply them in whatever manner they like. Instead, he is sent to 'teach' the Book. Then, since teaching the Book is not enough, he is also required to teach "Wisdom" which is something additional to the "Book". Still, this is not enough, therefore the Holy Prophet ﷺ has also to 'make the people pure', meaning thereby that the theoretical teaching of the Book and the 'Wisdom' must be followed by a practical training to enable the people to apply the Book and the wisdom in the way Allah requires them to apply.

This verse of the Holy Quran describes the following functions of the Holy Prophet ﷺ :

(a) He is the authority in the way the Holy Book has to be recited.

(b) He has the final word in the interpretation of the Book.

(c) He is the only source at which the wisdom based on divine guidance can be learned.

(d) He is entrusted with the practical training of the people to bring his teachings into practice.

These functions of the Holy Prophet ﷺ can never be carried out unless his teachings, both oral and practical, are held to be authoritative for his followers, and the Muslims who are given under his training are made bound to obey and follow him. The functions 'b' and 'c', namely, the teaching of the Book and Wisdom require that his 'sayings' should be binding on the followers, while the function 'd', the practical training, requires that his ' acts ' should be an example for the ummah, and the *ummah* should be bound to follow it.

It is not merely a logical inference from the verse of the Holy Quran quoted above, but it is also mentioned in express terms by the Holy Quran in a large number of verses which give the Muslims a mandatory command to obey and follow him. While doing so, the Holy Quran has used two different terms namely, the 'ita'ah' (to obey) and the 'ittiba' (to follow). The first term refers to the orders and sayings of the Holy Prophet ﷺ, while the second relates to his acts and practice. By ordering the Muslims both to ' obey ' and to 'follow' the Holy Prophet ﷺ the Holy Quran has given an authority to both his sayings and acts.

The obedience of the Messenger

It is in this background that the Holy Quran insists repeatedly on 'the obedience of the Prophet' so much so that it is mentioned side by side with, the obedience of Allah,

قُلْ أَطِيْعُوا اللهَ وَ الرَّسُوْلَ فَإِنْ تَوَلَّوْا فَإِنَّ اللهَ
لَا يُحِبُّ الْكَافِرِيْنَ

Say, ' Obey Allah and the Messenger but if they turn their backs Allah loves not the disbelievers'.

وَأَطِيْعُوا اللهَ وَالرَّسُوْلَ لَعَلَّكُمْ تُرْحَمُوْنَ (3:32)

And obey Allah and the Messenger so that you may be blessed. (3:132)

يَا أَيُّهَا الَّذِيْنَ آمَنُوْا أَطِيْعُوا اللهَ وَالرَّسُوْلَ وَأُولِي الأَمْرِ مِنْكُمْ

O those who believe, obey Allah and obey the Messenger and those in authority among you. (4:59)

وَأَطِيْعُوا اللهَ وَأَطِيْعُوا الرَّسُوْلَ وَاحْذَرُوا

And obey Allah and obey the Messenger and beware. (5:92)

فَاتَّقُوا اللهَ وَأَصْلِحُوْا ذَاتَ بَيْنِكُمْ وَأَطِيْعُوا اللهَ وَرَسُولَهُ إِنْ كُنْتُمْ مُؤْمِنِيْنَ

So, fear Allah and set things right between you and obey Allah and His Messenger if you are believers. (8:1)

يَا أَيُّهَا الَّذِيْنَ آمَنُوْا أَطِيْعُوا اللهَ وَرَسُوْلَهُ وَلاَ تَوَلَّوْا عَنْهُ وَأَنْتُمْ تَسْمَعُوْنَ

O those who believe, obey Allah and His Messenger and do not turn away from him, while you are listening (8:20)

وَأَطِيْعُوا اللهَ وَرَسُولَهُ وَلاَتَنَازَعُوا فَتَفْشَلُوا

And obey Allah and His Messenger and do not quarrel with each other, and so lose heart (8:46)

قُلْ أَطِيعُوا اللهَ وَأَطِيعُوا الرَّسُولَ فَإِنْ تَوَلَّوْا فَإِنَّمَا عَلَيْهِ مَا حُمِّلَ وَعَلَيْكُمْ مَّا حُمِّلْتُمْ وإِنْ تُطِيعُوهُ تَهْتَدُوْا

Say, 'Obey Allah and obey the Messenger; then, if you turn away, upon him rests what is laid on him, and upon you rests what is laid on you. If you obey him, you will be guided'. (24:54)

يَا أَيُّهَا الَّذِيْنَ آمَنُوْا أَطِيْعُوا اللهَ وَأَطِيْعُوا الرَّسُوْلَ وَلاَتُبْطِلُوا أَعْمَالَكُمْ

O those who believe, obey Allah and obey the Messenger and do not make your deeds vain. (47:33)

فَأَقِيْمُوا الصَّلاَةَ وَآتُوا الزَّكَاةَ وَأَطِيْعُوا اللهَ وَرَسُولَهُ

So, establish *salah* and pay *zakah* and obey Allah and His Messenger (58:13)

وَأَطِيْعُوا اللهَ وَأَطِيْعُوا الرَّسُوْلَ فَإِنْ تَوَلَّيْتُمْ فَإِنَّمَا عَلَى رَسُوْلِنَا الْبَلاَغُ الْمُبِيْنُ

And obey Allah and obey the Messenger, but if you turn your backs, Our Messenger has only to deliver the manifest message. (64:12)

In these verses 'the obedience of the Messenger' has been ordered as an obligatory command. There are other verses in which the results of the 'obedience of the Messenger' have been described. Here again the 'obedience of the Messenger' has been combined with 'the obedience of Allah':

وَمَن يُطِعِ اللهَ وَرَسُولَهُ يُدْخِلْهُ جَنَّاتٍ تَجْرِىْ مِنْ تَحْتِهَا الأَنْهَارُ

And whoever obeys Allah and His Messenger, Allah shall admit him in the Gardens underneath which rivers flow. (4:13)

The same words have been repeated in 48:17 also.

وَمَن يُطِعِ اللهَ وَالرَّسُولَ فَأُولَئِكَ مَعَ الَّذِيْنَ أَنْعَمَ اللهُ عَلَيْهِمْ

And whoever obeys Allah and the Messenger, - they are in the company of those whom Allah has blessed. (4:69)

وَمَا كَانَ قَوْلَ الْمُؤْمِنِيْنَ إِذَا دُعُوْا إِلَى اللهِ وَرَسُوْلِهِ لِيَحْكُمَ بَيْنَهُمْ إِلا أَنْ قَالُوْا سَمِعْنَا وَأَطَعْنَا وَأُولَئِكَ هُمُ الْمُفْلِحُوْنَ . وَمَن يُطِعِ اللهَ وَرَسُوْلَهُ وَيَخْشَ اللهَ وَيَتَّقْهِ فَأُولَئِكَ هُمُ الْفَائِزُوْنَ

All that the believers say, when they are called to Allah and His Messenger that he may judge between them, is that they say, 'We hear, and we obey: 'It is these who are successful. Whoever obeys Allah and His Messenger and fears Allah and has awe of Him - it is these who are the winners. (24:52)

وَمَن يُطِعِ اللهَ وَرَسُولَهُ فَقَدْ فَازَ فَوْزاً عَظِيْماً

And whoever obeys Allah and His Messenger, he has won a great success. (33:71)

اَلْمُؤْمِنُوْنَ وَالْمُؤْمِنَاتُ بَعْضُهُمْ أَوْلِيَاءُ بَعْضٍ يَأْمُرُوْنَ بِالْمَعْرُوفِ وَيَنْهَوْنَ عَنِ الْمُنْكَرِ وَيُقِيْمُوْنَ الصَّلاَةَ وَيُؤْتُوْنَ الزَّكَاةَ وَيُطِيْعُوْنَ اللهَ وَرَسُوْلَهُ أُولٰئِكَ سَيَرْحَمُهُمُ اللهُ، إِنَّ اللهَ عَزِيْزٌ حَكِيْمٌ

And the believers, men and women, a e friends of each other; they bid the fair and forbid the unfair; they establish *salah* and pay *zakah* and they obey Allah and His Messenger. These are those upon whom Allah shall have mercy; Allah is All - Mighty, All Wise. (9:71)

وَإِنْ تُطِيْعُوا اللهَ وَرَسُوْلَهُ لاَيَلِتْكُمْ مِّنْ أَعْمَالِكُمْ شَيْئًا

If you obey Allah and His Messenger, He will not diminish you anything of your deeds.(49:14)

The Holy Quran has also made it clear that 'the obedience of the prophet' is not a new principle, nor is it limited to the Holy Prophet Muhammad ﷺ. The same principle applied to all the former prophets who came before him:

وَمَاأَرْسَلْنَا مِنْ رَّسُوْلٍ إِلاَّ لِيُطَاعَ بِإِذْنِ اللهِ

And we sent no messenger, but that he should be obeyed by the leave of Allah. (4:64)

It is also clarified by the Holy Quran that the prophets are the spokesmen of Allah's pleasure. Hence, the obedience of the prophet is actually the obedience of Allah Himself.

وَمَن يُطِعِ الرَّسُوْلَ فَقَدْ أَطَاعَ اللهَ

And whoever obeys the Messenger, thereby obeys Allah.(41:80)

As the obedience of the Holy Prophet ﷺ has been stressed by the Holy Quran and has been combined with the 'obedience of Allah' in the same way his ' disobedience' has been warned against and is combined with the ' disobedience of Allah ':

وَمَن يَّعْصِ اللهَ وَرَسُوْلَهُ وَيَتَعَدَّ حُدُوْدَهُ يُدْخِلْهُ نَاراً خَالِداً فِيْهَا

And whoever disobeys Allah and His Messenger and transgresses His limits, He shall admit him to Fire where he shall remain for ever. (4:14)

وَمَنْ يَّعْصِ اللهَ وَرَسُوْلَهُ فَقَدْ ضَلَّ ضَلاَلاً مُّبِيْناً

And whoever disobeys Allah and His Messenger has gone astray into manifest error. (33:36)

وَمَن يَّعْصِ اللهَ وَرَسُولَهُ فَإِنَّ لَهُ نَارَ جَهَنَّمَ خَالِدِيْنَ فِيْهَا أَبَداً

And whoever disobeys Allah and His Messenger, for him there is the fire of *Jahannam*. There they shall remain for ever. (72:23)

وَمَن يُشَاقِقِ اللهَ وَرَسُولَهُ فَإِنَّ اللهَ شَدِيْدُ الْعِقَابِ

And whoever makes a breach with Allah and His Messenger, then Allah is severe in punishment. (8:13)

أَلَمْ يَعْلَمُوْا أَنَّهُ مَن يُحَادِدِ اللهَ وَرَسُوْلَهُ فَإِنَّ لَهُ نَارَ جَهَنَّمَ

Did they not come to know that whoever opposes Allah and His Messenger, for him there is the fire of *Jahannam*.? (9:63)

Thus, both positive and negative aspects of the obedience' have been dealt with in the Holy Quran and the 'obedience of the Holy Prophet ' in each one of these verses has been mentioned separately, alongwith the obedience of Allah:

It is noteworthy that whenever the 'obedience of Allah' is mentioned in the Holy Quran, it is always followed by the obedience of the Prophet' which has never been missed even in a single verse. There is no verse in the entire Book where the 'obedience of Allah' has been mentioned alone with no reference to the 'Obedience of the Messenger'.

On the contrary, there are some verses where only the 'obedience of the Messenger' has been mentioned, and there is no reference to the obedience of Allah':

وَأَقِيمُوا الصَّلَاةَ وَآتُوا الزَّكَاةَ وَأَطِيعُوا الرَّسُولَ لَعَلَّكُمْ تُرْحَمُونَ.

And establish *salah* and pay *Zakah* and obey the Prophet, so that you may be blessed. (24:56)

وَإِنْ تُطِيعُوهُ تَهْتَدُوا

And if you obey him (the Prophet), you shall find the right path. (24 : 54)

يَوْمَئِذٍ يَوَدُّ الَّذِينَ كَفَرُوا وَعَصَوُا الرَّسُولَ لَوْ تُسَوَّى بِهِمُ الْأَرْضُ

On that day those who disbelieved and disobeyed the Messenger will wish that the earth might be levelled with them. (4 : 42)

وَمَن يُشَاقِقِ الرَّسُوْلَ مِنْ بَعْدِ مَا تَبَيَّنَ لَهُ
الْهُدَى وَيَتَّبِعْ غَيْرَ سَبِيْلِ الْمُؤْمِنِيْنَ نُوَلِّهِ مَا تَوَلَّى
وَنُصْلِهِ جَهَنَّمَ وَسَاءَتْ مَصِيْراً.

> And whoever makes a breach with the Messenger after the right path has become clear to him, and follows a way other than that of the believers, We shall let him own what he chose and shall admit him in the *Jahannam*, and it is evil as a returning place. (4:115)

The reason for so much stress upon the 'obedience of the Prophet' is that the 'obedience of Allah' cannot be carried out except through the 'obedience of the Prophet'. Allah does not address each and every individual to tell him what He requires from him, as the Holy Quran puts it:

وَمَا كَانَ لِبَشَرٍ أَن يُكَلِّمَهُ اللهُ إِلاَّ وَحْيًا أَوْ مِن
وَّرَاءِ حِجَابٍ أَوْ يُرْسِلَ رَسُوْلاً فَيُوْحِيَ بِإِذْنِهِ مَا يَشَاءُ

> And it is not possible for a human being that Allah should speak to him, except by revelation, or from behind a curtain, or that He should send a messenger and he reveal by His leave what He wills. (42:51)

Therefore Allah conveys His injunctions only through His prophets, and his obedience cannot be carried out except by the obedience of the messengers. So, when a prophet bids something or forbids something, he does not do it in his private capacity, rather, he does so in the capacity of a messenger of Allah. When Allah Himself has given an express command 'to obey the Messenger', the obedience of the Prophet is actually the 'obedience of Allah', though in an indirect manner. This point has been clearly established by the Holy Quran in the following words:

وَمَن يُطِعِ الرَّسُوْلَ فَقَدْ أَطَاعَ اللهَ

And whoever obeys the Messenger, thereby obeys Allah. (4:80)

So, whenever only the 'obedience of the Messenger' has been mentioned in the Holy Quran it includes, without saying, the 'obedience of Allan' because the Messenger does not say anything in the capacity of a Messenger unless he is guided by a revelation from Allah:

وَمَا يَنطِقُ عَنِ الْهَوَى إِنْ هُوَ إِلاَّ وَحْيٌ يُوْحَى

And he (the Prophet) does not speak out of his own desire. It is not but a revelation revealed (to him) (53:3)

Looked at from this angle, the obedience of the Prophet ﷺ represents the obedience of Allah and the reference to the former always includes the latter . That is why the Holy Quran in some verses deemed it sufficient to refer to the obedience of the Messenger only, for the practical way to obey Allah is only to obey the prophet.

On the contrary, the Holy Quran did not deem it sufficient to refer to the 'obedience of Allah' without referring to the 'obedience of the Messenger', to remove even the remotest excuse for ignoring the 'obedience of the Prophet' and to leave no doubt whatsoever in the fact that the 'obedience of Allah' is not complete unless the 'obedience of the Prophet" is fully observed with all its implications.

Ittiba' (following) of the Prophet.

The second term used by the Holy Quran in respect of the prophets is the' *ittiba'*, i.e. to follow:

قُلْ إِنْ كُنْتُمْ تُحِبُّوْنَ اللهَ فَاتَّبِعُوْنِي يُحْبِبْكُمُ اللهُ
وَيَغْفِرْ لَكُمْ ذُنُوْبَكُمْ

Say, if you love Allah, follow me and Allah will love you and forgive you your sins (3:31)

اَلَّذِيْنَ يَتَّبِعُوْنَ الرَّسُوْلَ النَّبِيَّ الأُمِّيَّ الَّذِي
يَجِدُوْنَهُ مَكْتُوْبًا عِنْدَهُمْ فِي التَّوْرَاةِ وَالإِنْجِيْلِ

Those who follow the Messenger, the unlettered Prophet whom they find written down with them in the Torah and the Evangile... (7:157)

فَآمِنُوْا بِاللهِ وَرَسُوْلِهِ النَّبِيِّ الأُمِّيِّ الَّذِي يُؤْمِنُ
بِاللهِ وَكَلِمَاتِهِ وَاتَّبِعُوْهُ لَعَلَّكُمْ تَهْتَدُوْنَ.

Believe, then, in Allah and His Messenger, the unlettered Prophet, who believes in Allah and His words, and follow him so that you may be on the right path. (7:157)

لَقَدْ تَابَ اللهُ عَلَى النَّبِيِّ وَالْمُهَاجِرِيْنَ وَالأَنْصَارِ
الَّذِيْنَ اتَّبَعُوْهُ فِي سَاعَةِ الْعُسْرَةِ

Allah has surely relented towards the Prophet and the Emigrants and the Helpers who followed him in an hour of difficulty (9:117)

يَا أَيُّهَا النَّبِيُّ حَسْبُكَ اللهُ وَمَنِ اتَّبَعَكَ مِنَ
الْمُؤْمِنِيْنَ

O Prophet, sufficient to you is Allah and those who followed you of the believers (8:64)

رَبَّنَا آمَنَّا بِمَا أَنزَلْتَ وَاتَّبَعْنَا الرَّسُوْلَ فَاكْتُبْنَا مَعَ الشَّاهِدِيْنَ .

(The believers say:) Our Lord, we have come to believe in what You revealed, and followed the Messenger. So, write us among those who bear witness. (3:53)

قُلْ هَذِهِ سَبِيْلِي أَدْعُو إِلَى اللهِ عَلَى بَصِيْرَةٍ أَنَا وَمَنْ اتَّبَعَنِي

Say, " This is my way. I call to Allah with sure knowledge, I and whoever follows me." (12:108)

إِنَّ أَوْلَى النَّاسِ بِإِبْرَاهِيْمَ لَلَّذِيْنَ اتَّبَعُوْهُ

The closest of the people to Ibrahim are those who follow him. (3:68)

وَجَعَلْنَا فِي قُلُوْبِ الَّذِيْنَ اتَّبَعُوْهُ رَأْفَةً وَرَحْمَةً

And We set in the hearts of those who followed him (Jesus) tenderness and mercy (57:27)

وَأَنْذِرِ النَّاسَ يَوْمَ يَأْتِيْهِمُ الْعَذَابُ فَيَقُوْلُ الَّذِيْنَ ظَلَمُوْا رَبَّنَا أَخِّرْنَا إِلَى أَجَلٍ قَرِيْبٍ نُجِبْ دَعْوَتَكَ وَنَتَّبِعِ الرُّسُلَ . (إبراهيم: ٤٤)

And warn the people of the day when the punishment comes on them and those who did evil shall say , "Our Lord, defer us to a near term; and we shall respond to Your call and shall follow the messengers". (14:44)

وما جعَلنا القبْلةَ الّتي كُنْتَ عَلَيْها إلا لِنَعْلَمَ مَن يَتَّبِع الرّسولَ مِمَّن يَنْقَلِبُ على عَقِبَيه

And We did not appoint the Qiblah on which you were earlier, but that We might know the people who follow the Messenger, as distinct from those who turn back on their heels (2:143)

قالَ يا قَومِ اتَّبِعوا المُرْسَلِينَ (يس : ٢٠)

He said, 'My people, follow the messengers'. (36:20)

وإنَّ رَبَّكُمُ الرَّحمنُ فاتَّبِعوني و أطيعوا أمْري

(طه : ٩٠)

(Moses said:) And your Lord is the 'Rahman' (the All-Merciful). So, follow me and obey my command. (20:90)

فَقالوا أبَشَراً مِنّا واحِداً نَتَّبِعُه إنّا إذا لفي ضَلالٍ وسُعُرٍ (القمر : ٢٤)

So, they (the disbelievers) said, 'Shall we follow a single human being from among us? Then, indeed we should be in error and insanity'. (54:24)

All these verses, with different styles and connotations, lay a strong emphasis on the necessity of 'following the prophets', and indicate that whoever believes in a prophet is bound to 'follow' him. The reason is obvious. The prophets are sent to the people to set a practical example of what they teach and preach. Their message is not confined to their oral teachings . Their acts are equally important in any effort to discover, learn and follow the right way of living. The Holy Quran is quite explicit on this point when it was said in Surah al - Ahzab:

لَقَد كانَ لَكُم في رسولِ اللهِ أُسْوَةٌ حَسَنَةٌ لِمَن كانَ يَرْجُو اللّهَ واليَومَ الآخِرَ وذَكَرَ اللهَ كَثيراً

(الأحزاب : ٢١)

There is surely a good example for you in the Messenger of Allah, for the one who hopes (to meet) Allah and the Hereafter, and remembers Allah abundantly." (33:21)

It is an established fact that mere theoretical education cannot be sufficient for reforming a people. The natural way of reformation is to set a practical example which people may follow. Mere reading of books cannot make a person perfect in a science or art, unless he is simultaneously trained by a senior scholar or a skillful artist of that field. If somebody studies the books of medical science, but does not work under the supervision of an experienced doctor, he despite his thorough study, cannot claim to serve as a doctor nor can such a person be allowed to play with the lives of the patients.

If somebody studies books of law, he cannot claim to be a lawyer unless he acquires a practical training from a senior lawyer and remains for a considerable time under his juniorship.

Even a plain enthusiast who wants to cook a good meal cannot do so perfectly by merely studying the books written on the subject, although all the ingredients required for cooking the food are mentioned in the book and even the minute details of the process are fully described. But a person who has never cooked that meal before cannot prepare it just right and perfect with the sole help of a cook - book unless he is practically trained by some expert. That expert sets a practical example for him and he, by following the example, gradually learns how to cook that good meal.

It clearly shows that human beings are always in need of a practical example in order to learn an important subject. The same is true in the matter of religious teaching and training.

That is why Allah did not choose to send the divine books only. He always sent a messenger with the book. There are many prophets who came without a new divine book. But there is no divine book sent down without a prophet. The disbelievers of Makkah, too, demanded many times that the Book should be revealed to them without the mediation of the Holy Prophet ﷺ. But the demand was rejected and the Book was sent through the Holy Prophet ﷺ.

The reason is obvious. Humanity did not need a divine book only. It also needed a teacher who could teach them the contents of the Book. It also needed an instructor who could train them and could set a practical example for them without which they could not benefit from the Book in their practical life. It was for this reason that the Holy Prophet ﷺ was sent with a clear direction to all human beings that they are bound to obey and follow him and to learn the details of Allah's pleasure through the practical example set before them by him. It was also clarified in the foregoing verse of the Holy Book that the 'obedience of the Messenger' is actually the 'obedience of Allah' and that the latter cannot be carried out except through the former, because whatever the Holy Prophet ﷺ says or does in the capacity of a prophet is based on the revelation received by him from Allah. Thus, his sayings and his acts both, even though they are not contained in the Holy Quran, are inspired or confirmed by the divine revelation.

TWO KINDS OF REVELATION

It follows from the foregoing discussion that the revelation the Holy Prophet ﷺ receives from Allah is of two different kinds:

(i) the revelation of the Quran, the Holy Book, named in the Islamic terminology as al-wahy al-matluww (the recited revelation i.e., the revelation which can be recited in the prayers). This kind of revelation is confined to the verses of the Holy Quran and is written verbally in its folds.

(ii) the revelation received by the Holy Prophet ﷺ from time to time to let him know the pleasure of Allah in day -to-day affairs and the details of the principles laid down in the Holy Quran with their correct interpretation. This kind of revelation is called al-wahy ghair-al-matluww (the unrecited revelation). This kind of revelation is not conveyed to the people verbally. It has been demonstrated through the sayings and acts of the Holy Prophet ﷺ .

THE SECOND KIND OF REVELATION PROVED BY THE HOLY QURAN.

This second kind of revelation is not contained in the Holy Quran, but the Holy Quran itself not only refers to it frequently but attributes its contents to Allah Almighty. Some verses of the Holy Book are reproduced below which clearly prove that the 'revelation' is not confined to the Holy Quran, but there is another kind of '*wahy*' which does not form part of the "Holy Book", yet it is the revelation from Allah Almighty:

The Holy Quran says:

وما جَعَلنا القِبْلَةَ الّتي كُنْتَ عَلَيْها إلا لِنَعْلَمَ مَن يَتَّبِعِ الرّسولَ مِمَّن يَنْقَلِبُ على عَقِبَيه

And We did not appoint the Qiblah on which you were earlier but that We might know the people who follow the Messenger as distinct from those who turn back on their heels. (2:143)

In order to understand the verse, it is necessary to know the background in which it was revealed:

In the early days of *Madani* life, after the Holy Prophet's migration to *Madinah*, the Muslims were ordered to direct their faces in prayers towards *Bytul-Maqdis* (Jerusalem) which had been appointed as *Qiblah* of the Muslims. Upto seventeen months the Muslims had been observing the Bytul-Maqdis as their *Qiblah*. It was after seventeen months that the Holy Quran abrogated the earlier order and the Muslims were required to observe the Holy Mosque of Makkah as their *Qiblah* and turn their faces towards it while praying. The following verse was revealed to appoint the new *Qiblah*:

فَوَلِّ وَجْهَكَ شَطرَ المَسْجِدِ الحَرام

So, turn your face towards Al-Masjid-al-Haram. (2:144)

This new order was criticised by some disbelievers and they objected on it as to why the Bytul-Maqdis was appointed as *Qiblah* earlier. The above quoted verse (2:143) was revealed to answer this objection. The answer was that the appointment of the former *Qiblah* was in order to test the people whether or not they follow the Messenger. To quote the verse again:

" And We did not appoint the *Qiblah* on which you were earlier (i.e. Bytul - Maqdis) but that We might know the people who follow the Messenger......."

Here the appointment of the previous *Qiblah* has been attributed to Allah Almighty which is a clear indication to the fact that the appointment of Bytul - Maqdis as Qiblah was done by the order of Allah Almighty Himself. But this order is nowhere in the Holy Quran, and there is no verse in the Holy Book which directs the turning of faces towards Bytul-Maqdis. This order was given to Muslims by the Holy Prophet ﷺ with no reference to any verse of the Holy Quran. Still, this order was mentioned by the Holy Quran in the above quoted verse as the order of Allah: The words:

"We did not appoint the Qiblah" instead of the words:

"The Holy Prophet did not" ....are too clear on this point to need more explanation.

This statement of the Holy Quran, thus, evidently proves that the previous order given by the Holy Prophet ﷺ was based on a revelation which did not form part of the Book. And this is exactly the ' Unrecited revelation '. The verse of the Holy Quran (2:143) quoted above proves the following facts:

(a) the Holy Prophet used to receive some revelations which are not contained in the Holy Quran.

(b) These revelations were from Allah Almighty, so much so that the orders based on such revelations were attributed to Allah Almighty.

(c) The orders based on such revelation were as binding on the believers as the orders of the first kind of revelations i.e., the verses of Holy Quran.

(d) These orders were sometimes given so as to test whether or not the Muslims follow the Messenger ﷺ irrespective of the question that his orders are contained in the Holy Quran or not.

2. In the beginning one of the rules followed by the Muslims in respect of the fasts of Ramadan was that even a short nap after *iftar* (breaking of a fast) would nullify the permissibility of having sexual intercourse with one's wife. So, if someone would sleep for a short while after iftar and wake up again, he would lose the opportunity of sleeping with his wife during the rest of the night, despite that the fast was over. This rule was prescribed by the Holy Prophet ﷺ and was not contained in the Holy Quran. But some Muslims broke the rule by sleeping with their wives after having a post-iftar nap. Referring to these events, the Holy Quran first admonishes those people who did not follow the rule. Then, by abrogating the same allows the Muslims in future to sleep with their wives even when they had a nap after iftar. In this context the Holy Quran says:

أُحِلَّ لَكُم لَيْلَةَ الصِّيامِ الرَّفَثُ إلى نِساءِكُم هُنَّ لِباسٌ لَكُم و أَنْتُم لِباسٌ لَهُنَّ عَلِمَ اللّهُ أَنَّكُم كُنْتُم تَخْتانونَ أَنْفُسَكُم فَتابَ عَلَيكُم وعَفا عَنْكُم ، فالآنَ باشِرُوهُنَّ وابْتَغوا ما كَتَبَ اللهُ لَكُم حتّى يَتَبَيَّنَ لَكُم الخَيْطُ الأَبْيَضُ مِنَ الخَيْطِ الأَسْوَدِ مِنَ الفَجْرِ ، ثُمَّ أَتِمُّوا الصِّيامَ إلى اللَّيْلِ (البقرة : ١٨٧)

It is made lawful for you, in the nights of fasts, to have sex with your women. They are a cover for you, and you are a cover for them. Allah knew that you were betraying yourselves; so, He relented towards you and pardoned you. So, now you can have sexual intimacy with them, and seek what Allah has destined for you, and eat and drink until the white thread of the dawn becomes distinct from the black thread; then complete the fasts upto the night. (2: 187)

The following points with respect to this verse are worth consideration:

(a) The verse confirms that having sex during the nights of 'Ramadan' was not lawful before.

(b) The people who had sex during the nights of Ramadan before this verse was revealed, are admonished by describing their act as 'betraying themselves'.

(c) The words, 'so He relented towards you and pardored you', indicate that their sexual act was a sin, because 'relenting' and 'pardoning' occur only after a person commits a sin.

(d) The words 'so now you can have sexual intimacy with them' denote that it is only now that the sexual act during the nights of Ramadan has been made lawful.

All these points confirm the fact that the earlier prohibition of having sexual intercourse during the nights of Ramadan was validly made by a competent authority, and the Muslims were bound to abide by it.

But there is no verse in the Holy Quran to convey this prohibition. It was enforced only by the Holy Prophet ﷺ . Still, the Holy Quran not only confirms it , but also treats it as if it were in its own words. It is due to the fact that the Holy Prophet ﷺ did not enforce this prohibition by his own will, it was rather, based on a revelation of Allah Almighty which is not contained in the Holy Quran.

Looked at from this angle, this verse on the one hand proves that there is a revelation which does not form part of the Holy Quran , and on the other hand, it reaffirms the status of the

Holy Prophet ﷺ as a law-giver, and that his injunctions, both orders and prohibitions, are binding on the Muslims.

3. On the accasion of the battle of Uhud, some Quranic verses were revealed to make the Muslims recall the events of the Battle of Badr: How Allah helped them and how He promised them to send the angels to their aid, and how He actually did so. These verses are as under:

لَقَد نَصَرَكُمُ اللّهُ بِبَدْرٍ وَ أَنتُم أَذِلَّةٌ فاتَّقوا الله
لَعَلَّكُم تَشْكُرونَ إذْ تَقُولُ لِلمُؤمِنِينَ أ لَن يَكْفِيَكُم
أن يُمِدَّكُم رَبُّكُم بِثَلاثَةِ آلافٍ مِنَ المَلائِكَةِ مُنْزَلِين
بلى إنْ تَصْبِروا و تَتَّقوا ويأتوكُم مِن فَورِهِم هذا
يُمْدِدكُم رَبُّكُم بِخَمسَةِ آلافٍ من المَلائكَة
مُسَوِّمِينَ. وما جَعَلَهُ الله إلا بُشرَى لَكم و لِتَطمَئِنَّ
قُلوبُكُم بِهِ وما النَّصرُ إلا من عِندِ الله العَزيزِ
الحَكيم. (آل عمران ، ١٢٣ - ١٢٥)

Allah has certainly helped you at Badr while you were weak. So, fear Allah, so that you may be grateful. When you (O Prophet) were saying to the believers, "Shall it not suffice you that your Lord shall aid you with three thousand angels being sent down? Why not? If you observe patience and fear Allah and they come to you in this their heat, your Lord shall aid you with five thousand angels having distinct marks". *And Allah did not make it but a good news for you* so that your hearts might be satisfied. And there is no help but from Allah, the All-Mighty, the All-Wise." (3: 123,126)

The italicised sentence of these verses attributes the good news of the aid of angels to Allah Almighty, meaning thereby that the good news of this aid was given by Allah Himself. But this good news given at the time of Badr is nowhere available in the Holy Quran. In other words, there is no verse in the Holy Book revealed during the battle of Badr which implies the good news of the aid of the angels. What is quoted above is only a reference of that news, made at the time of a later battle, and it is expressly mentioned in this verse that the goodnews was given by the Holy Prophet ﷺ. Still, the news is attributed to Allah.

Thus, it is another example where the words of the Holy Prophet ﷺ are held to be the words of Allah. There is no reason for this expression other than that the words of the Prophet ﷺ were inspired by a special revelation, not contained in the Holy Quran, and this is what is called the 'unrecited revelation'.

4. Referring to the battle of Uhud at another occasion, the Holy Quran says,

و إذ يَعِدُكُم الله إحْدَى الطَّائِفَتَينِ أنَّها لَكُم

(الأنفال : ٧)

And when Allah promised you that one of the two groups shall be for you (8:7)

One of the two parties referred to in this verse was the commercial caravan of Abu Sufyan, coming from Syria, and the other group was the army of the Makkan disbelievers, led by Abu Jahl. The above verse says that Allah had promised the believers that they would triumph over one of these two groups. The Muslims, in fact, won the battle against the latter, namely, the army of Abu Jahl.

The point worth consideration here is that the promise of Allah to give the Muslims victory against any of the two groups is not there in the Holy Quran. This promise was conveyed to the

Muslims by the Holy Prophet ﷺ without any reference to any verse of the Holy Quran. Still the verse quoted above attributes the promise to Allah, and not to the Holy Prophet ﷺ

The only conclusion derivable from this is that the promise was received by the Holy Prophet ﷺ through an 'unrecited revelation'. Hence, it is attributed to Allah. Guided by this revelation, the Holy Prophet ﷺ conveyed the promise to his companions.

Thus, it is another proof of the existence of a kind of revelation which is not contained in the Holy Quran and is called the 'unrecited revelation'.

5. Once the Holy Prophet ﷺ told a secret to one of his wives. She disclosed the secret to some other person. When the Holy Prophet came to know that the secret has been disclosed by his wife, he sought an explanation from her. She asked him as to who told him about the disclosure. The Holy Prophet ﷺ replied that he was informed about it by Allah Almighty.

This event has been mentioned by the Holy Quran in the following words:

وإذ أَسَرَّ النَّبِيُّ إلى بَعْضِ أَزْوَاجِهِ حَدِيثاً فَلَمَّا
نَبَّأَتْ بِهِ و أَظْهَرَهُ اللهُ عليه عَرَّفَ بعضَه وأعرَضَ عن
بَعْضٍ فَلَمَّا نَبَّأَهَا به قالَتْ مَنْ أَنبَأَكَ هذا قالَ نَبَّأَنِي
العَلِيمُ الخَبِيرُ. (التحريم : ٣)

"And when the Prophet told one of his wives about a matter secretly: then, when she told about it, *and Allah has disclosed it to him,* he made known some part of it, and turned aside from some part; then, when he told her about it, she said, " Who told you this"? He said, ' *I was told by the All -Knowing, the All -Aware.*

The italicised sentences of this verse are quite clear in that Allah has told the Holy Prophet ﷺ about the disclosure of the secret. This is also not mentioned anywhere in the Holy Quran. So, it is another concrete example where the Holy Prophet ﷺ received some revelation from Allah other than the one contained in the Holy Quran. This is exactly the 'unrecited revelation'.

6. During the seige of Banu Nadir, the famous tribe of the Jews in Medinah, some Muslims had cut down date-trees from around the fort to compel the enemy to surrender. After the war was over, some Jews objected to the cutting trees. The Holy Quran has answered the objection in the following words:

ما قَطَعْتُم مِن لِينَةٍ أو تَرَكْتُموها قائمَةً على أصولِها فَبِإذنِ الله . (الحشر : ٥)

Whatever date-trees you cut down, or left standing upon their roots, that was by the leave of Allah (59:5)

It has been very directly mentioned in this verse that the Muslims cut down the trees with a leave from Allah. But nobody can point out to any verse in the Holy Quran to the effect that the cutting of trees during the war is allowed. The question is: from where did the Muslims acquire this leave from Allah? There is no answer to this question except that the leave of Allah had been conveyed to them by the Holy Prophet ﷺ and he received it through 'unrecited revelation'.

7. It is well known that the Holy Prophet ﷺ had adopted Sayyidna Zaid b. Harithah as his son. He married Zainab daughter of Jahsh. After some time their relations began to be strained and, ultimately, he divorced her. In the days of *Jahiliyyah* an adopted son was treated as a real son in all respects,

and for all purposes. The Holy Quran, on the other hand, declared that the adopted sons cannot be treated as the real ones.

To eradicate the *Jahili* concept of the adopted son, Allah Almighty ordered the Holy Prophet ﷺ that he should marry Zainab after her having been divorced by his adopted son, Zaid ibn Harithah. The Holy Prophet ﷺ was a bit reluctant in the beginning, for, according to the prevalent custom, it was treated a shameful act to marry the divorced wife of one's adopted son. But when the Holy Prophet ﷺ received a concrete order from Allah, he married her.

This event has been mentioned by the Holy Quran in the following words :

و إذ تَقُولُ لِلّذي أنْعَمَ اللهُ عليه و أنْعَمْتَ عليه
أمْسِكْ عليكَ زَوجَكَ واتّقِ اللهَ ، وتُخْفي في نَفْسِكَ ما
اللهُ مُبْديهِ و تَخْشَى الناسَ واللهُ أحَقُّ أن تخشاه
فلَمّا قَضَى زَيدٌ منها وطَراً زوَّجْناكَها لِكَيلا يَكونَ
على المؤمنينَ حَرَجٌ في أزْواجِ أدْعِيائِهِم إذا قَضَوا
مِنهنَّ وطَرا وكانَ أمرُ اللهِ مَفْعولا .

(الأحزاب ، ٣٧)

When you were saying to the one whom Allah had blessed and whom you had blessed, (i.e. Zaid before he divorced Zainab), "Keep to you your wife and fear Allah," and you were hiding in your heart what Allah was to disclose and you were fearing people, and Allah has more right to be feared by you. So, when Zaid finished with her, We made you marry her, so that there may remain no restriction on the believers in respect of the wives of their adopted sons when they have finished with them. And the order of Allah had to be done. (33:37)

Here the words, *'you were hiding in your heart what Allah was to disclose'* refer to the fact that Allah had informed the Holy Prophet ﷺ that he will marry Zainab after she is divorced by Zaid. The Holy Prophet ﷺ knew that, ultimately, she is going to be divorced by Zaid, but, out of shame, he could not disclose it and when Zaid consulted him in the matter, he advised him to keep to his wife and not to divorce her.

From this it follows that the Holy Prophet ﷺ had been foretold by Allah that Zainab was going to be divorced by her husband. But this information is not contained in the Holy Quran. It was given to him through an unrecited revelation.

The second sentence is more significant in the context, that is, "We made you marry her." Here Allah Almighty declares that the marriage between the Holy Prophet ﷺ and Sayyidah Zainab was contracted by an order of Allah. This order is nowhere mentioned in the Holy Quran. Still, the Holy Quran affirms it. This is another confirmation of an order conveyed to the Holy Prophet ﷺ through an 'unrecited revelation'.

8. The Holy Quran has repeatedly ordered the Muslims to establish salah (the prayer) and to be steadfast in it. In the following verse, after repeating the same order, the Holy Quran gives a special concession to the Muslims that in the state of war, when they fear an attack from their enemy, they can perform the prayer in whatever way they can, either riding on horses or camels or walking on their feet. But after the danger of the enemy is over, they are ordered to perform the prayer in its normal way. This principle has been laid down in the following words:

حافظوا على الصّلوات والصلاة الوُسطى و
قوموا لله قانتين . فإن خفتم فرجالا أو رُكباناً فإذا

أمِنتُم فاذكُروا الله كما علَّمَكُم .

(البقرة : ٢٣٩ , ٢٤٠)

Take due care of all the prayers and the middle prayer, and stand before Allah in total devotion. But if you are in fear, then (pray) on foot or riding, but when you are in peace, then recite the name of Allah in the way He taught you. (2:239,240)

A number of points are worth consideration in these verses:

Firstly, the verse assumes that there are more than one prayers obligatory on the Muslims, but the exact number of the prayers has not been given, neither in this verse nor at any other place in the Holy Quran. That the number of obligatory prayers is five is only mentioned by the Holy Prophet ﷺ. The Holy Quran by saying '*Take due care of all the prayers*' confirms what the Holy Prophet ﷺ prescribed for the Muslims.

Secondly, the verse lays special emphasis on the "Middle Prayer', but does not define it. The definition has been left to the Holy Prophet ﷺ.

Thirdly, the most important sentence in relation to our subject is , '<u>when you are in peace, then, recite the name of Allah in the way He taught you</u>'. It goes without saying that the 'recitation of the name of Allah' means here ' to perform the prayer' as the context does not permit any other meaning.

Now, the Holy Quran directs the Muslims that in the state of peace they should perform the prayer in its normal way which has been taught to them by Allah. It is an express indication that the normal way of performing prayers has been taught to the Muslims by Allah Himself. But no such way has ever been mentioned in the Holy Quran. There is no verse in the Holy Book mentioning the detailed way of performing prayer. It is only the Holy Prophet ﷺ who educated the Muslims as to how they are to perform it. But the Holy Quran holds the teaching of the Holy Prophet to be the teaching of Allah.

It means that Allah has taught the way of prayer to the Holy Prophet ﷺ through some 'unrecited revelation' not contained in the Holy Quran, and the Holy Prophet ﷺ taught it to the Muslims. Thus, the Muslims have been taught by Allah through the teaching of the Holy Prophet ﷺ. However, the teaching of the Holy Prophet ﷺ is described in the Holy verse as the teaching of Allah, because it was based on the 'unrecited revelation'.

9. Certain hypocrites had not accompanied the Holy Prophet ﷺ in the expedition of Hudaibiyah. After that, when the Muslims resolved to proceed to the battle of Khyber, the Holy Prophet ﷺ declared that only the participants of Hudaibiyah shall be entitled to accompany him on this journey. The hypocrites who did not go to Hudaibiyah were now interested in their participation in the battle of Khyber, because, according to their anticipation, the Muslims were expected to gain from there sizeable spoils which the hypocrites wanted to share. But the Holy Prophet ﷺ, inspite of their requests, did not allow them to participate in the battle.

This event has been referred to in the following verse of the Holy Quran :

سَيَقُولُ الْمُخَلَّفُونَ إِذَا انطَلَقْتُمْ إِلَى مَغَانِمَ
لِتَأْخُذُوهَا ذَرُونَا نَتَّبِعْكُمْ يُرِيدُونَ أَن يُبَدِّلُوا كَلَامَ اللهِ
قُلْ لَن تَتَّبِعُونَا كَذَلِكُمْ قَالَ اللهُ مِن قَبْلُ . (الفتح ١٥)

"Those remaining behind will say, when you set forth after spoils to acquire them, 'Let us follow you' *desiring to change the words of Allah. Say, 'You shall not follow us; so Allah has said earlier.'* (48:15)

The words in italics indicate that there was a previous word of Allah barring the participation of the hypocrites in the battle of Khyber, and confining the battle to the participants of Hudaibiyah. But no such word exists anywhere in the Holy Quran. It was only a prophetic order. Still, Allah Almighty describes it as His Own word. The reason is obvious. The Prophetic order was based on the order of Allah received by him through some 'unrecited revelation' which is not found in the Holy Quran. Yet, it was a revelation, as certain as any word of Allah.

10. In the early days of his Prophethood, when the Holy Prophet ﷺ received the verses of the Holy Quran revealed to him, he used to recite the same simultaneously, lest he should forget them. It was a strenuous exercise for him, because he felt it was much too difficult to listen to the revelation, to understand it correctly, and to learn it by heart, all at the same time. Allah Almighty relieved him from this burden when He revealed the following verses of the Holy Quran:

لا تُحَرِّكْ به لِسانَكَ لِتَعْجَلَ به إنَّ علينا جَمْعَه

وقرآنَه فإذا قَرأناه فاتَّبع قرآنَه ثمَّ إنَّ علينا بيانَه .

Move not your tongue with it in order to hasten it. It is on Us to gather it (in your heart) and to recite it. So, when We read it, follow its reading. *Then it is on Us to explain it.* (75:16,19)

In the last sentence, Allah Almighty has promised the Holy Prophet ﷺ to explain the verses of the Holy Quran to him. It is evident that this explanation is something separate from the Holy Quran itself. It is not the Holy Quran. It is its explanation or its exegesis. Therefore, it should necessarily be in some other form, distinct from the words of the Holy Book. And this is exactly what is meant by the 'unrecited revelation'. But the two kinds of revelation, though different in their form, are both revealed to the Holy Prophet ﷺ, both are from Allah, and both are to be believed and obeyed by the Muslims.

11. The Holy Quran says to the Holy Prophet ﷺ :

وَ لوأنزَلَ اللهُ عليكَ الكِتابَ والحِكْمَةَ وعَلَّمَكَ ما لَم تَكُن تَعْلَم وكانَ فَضْلُ اللهِ عليكَ عظيماً

(النساء ۱۱۳)

And Allah has revealed upon you the Book and the wisdom, and has taught you what you did not know, and the grace of Allah upon you has been great. (4:113)

In this verse the revelation of the Wisdom has been mentioned as separate from the revelation of the Book. It indicates that the wisdom referred to here is something additional to the Holy Quran, and it has also been revealed to the Holy Prophet ﷺ by Allah Almighty. Then the Holy Quran proceeds to say :

"And (Allah) has taught you what you did not know".

It means that Allah has not only revealed the Book, but has also revealed the Wisdom, and also taught the Holy Prophet ﷺ what he did not know before. This teaching includes all kinds of directions given by Him to his Prophet, either through the Holy Book or through some 'unrecited revelation' in the light of which the Holy Prophet ﷺ performed his functions as a messenger of Allah.

12. The Holy Quran has summarised the various kinds of revelation in the following words:

ما كانَ لِبَشَرٍ أن يُكَلِّمَه اللهُ إلا وحيا أو مِن وراء حِجابٍ أو يُرْسِلَ رَسولا فيُوحيَ بإذنِه ما يشاءُ

(الشورى ۵۱)

And it is not possible for a human being that Allah should speak to him, except by way of revelation, or from behind a curtain, or that He should send a messenger and he reveals by His leave what He wills".(42:51)

Now, out of these three modes, the revelation of the Holy Quran was carried out through the third one, namely, through an angel who is identified in the verse by the word, 'messenger'. It is clearly settled by some other verses:

قُلْ مَنْ كانَ عَدُوّاً لِجبريلَ فإنّه نَزَّله على قَلبِكَ

بإذنِ اللهِ (البقرة : ٩٧)

Say, whoever be an enemy to Jibril (*Gabriel*, the angel)-- it is he who has brought it (the Quran) down upon your heart by the permission of Allah (2:97)

وإنّه لَتَنْزيلُ رَبِّ العلمينَ نَزَلَ به الرُوحُ الأمينُ

على قَلبِكَ لِتَكونَ من المُنْذِرينَ بِلِسانٍ عَرَبيٍّ مُبينٍ

(الشعراء : ١٩٢- ١٩٥)

And truly, it (the Quran) is the revelation of the Lord of the worlds, brought down by the Faithful Spirit upon your heart, that you may be one of the warners, in a clear Arabic tongue. (26:129,195)

These verses are quite explicit on the point that the Holy Quran has been revealed through an angel, named in the first verse as *Jibril*, and in the second one as the Faithful Spirit; but the verse (42:51) quoted above describes that there are two more ways of revelation. These two modes have also been used in the case of the Holy Prophet ﷺ. It means that the revelation sent down to the Holy Prophet was not confined to the Holy Quran, but there were other revelations, too. These revelations are termed as 'unrecited revelation'.

These are sixteen verses, which affirm not only the existence of the 'unrecited revelation' but also its reliability and authenticity, and its binding nature. It is not intended here to produce all the material available in the Holy Quran to establish this kind of revelation. The purpose was to give some examples only, which has, perhaps, been substantially served. But before proceeding further, it will be useful to recollect and summarise the conclusions that stand proved in the light of the Holy Quran as discussed above:

(1) The function of the Holy Prophet ﷺ like other prophets is not only to convey the divine Book. He is also to teach the Book, to teach the wisdom and to make people pure by training them practically.

(2) The 'Obedience of the Holy Prophet' ﷺ, is as necessary as the obedience of Allah; because the latter has always been mentioned in the Holy Quran combined with the former.

(3) 'The Obedience of the Holy Prophet' ﷺ in practical terms is 'the obedience of Allah'; and the latter cannot be carried out except through the former.

(4) The Muslims are bound not only to obey the Holy Prophet, but they are also under an obligation to follow him.

(5) Whatever the Holy Prophet ﷺ says or does in his capacity of a Messenger is always based on, or confirmed by, a revelation from Allah.

(6) This revelation is sometimes contained in the Holy Quran and called the recited revelation, and sometimes it is sent down in addition to the Holy Quran, and the same is termed as 'unrecited revelation'.

The obedience of the Prophet as distinct from the obedience of a ruler

From the above conclusions, which are based purely on the verses of the Holy Quran, another possiblity, often overemphasized by some quarters while opposing the authority of the sunnah, is completely ruled out. It is sometimes said that the Holy Quran, when it ordains the obedience of the Holy Prophet ﷺ, means his obedience in the capacity of a ruler or a head of the state, and not in the capacity of a prophet. Since the Holy Prophet ﷺ was also a ruler of the Muslims, they were ordered to 'obey' and 'follow' him. But after he passed away, his personal obedience is no more necessary. Now, whoever takes over the rule shall stand for the Holy Prophet ﷺ in the matter of obedience, and the Muslims should follow him.

This fallacy is based on the misconception that the Holy Prophet ﷺ was ordered to be obeyed in his capacity of a ruler, and not in the capacity of a prophet or messenger.

But the verses already quoted leave no room for this misconception. The reasons are as under:

(1) Wherever the Holy Quran has directed toward the 'obedience of the Holy Prophet' it has always referred to the 'obedience of the Messenger' and not to the obedience of the ruler', nor to the obedience of 'Muhammad' ﷺ in his private capacity. It clearly indicates that he must be obeyed on account of his being a messenger.

When I say, to someone, 'obey your father', it means that his being father is the basic cause of his being obeyed. If I say, 'obey your teacher', it is evident that his being teacher is the cause of his obedience being due. Nobody can reasonably interpret these sentences conversely. So, when Allah Almighty says 'Obey the Messenger' how can it be reasonable to say that his messengership is not the cause of his obedience?

(2) At one occasion, at least, the Holy Quran has removed even the remotest possibility of this wrong interpretation, when it said:

يا أيُها الَّذينَ آمنوا أطِيْعُوا اللهَ وَأطِيْعُوا الرَّسُوْلَ وأولي الأمرِ مِنكُم

(النساء ، ٥٩)

O those who believe, obey Allah and obey the Messenger and those in authority among you (4:59)

Here, the obedience of the messenger has been separated and distinguished from that of the ruling authorities, which means that the 'messenger ' and 'those in authority' both are to be obeyed in their different capacities.

It is important to note that in the case of the Holy Prophet ﷺ both the capacities were combined in him. He was a Messenger as well as a ruler. Therefore, if the Holy Quran intended to restrict the obedience of the Holy Prophet to his lifetime only, it could easily be said, 'Obey Muhammad ﷺ '. But by avoiding this expression, the Holy Quran explicitly differentiated between his two capacities, and mentioned each of them separately to remove even the slightest apprehension of this misconception, and thus left no room for confusing one capacity with the other.

Moreover, there is another point to note in this verse. The word 'Messenger' used here is in singular, while the phrase 'those in authority', is in plural. This is to signify that the Holy Prophet ﷺ is the last messenger after whom no prophet will come. So, his obedience as a prophet shall always be confined to himself alone. Nobody can share with him in this obedience in future. On the other hand, the ruling authorities shall be in a large number, coming one after the other. This kind of obedience is not restricted to the ruler present at the time of revelation; it, rather, extends to all the ruling authorities coming after him.

(3) It has been established earlier that the obedience of the Holy Prophet ﷺ was based on the 'unrecited revelation' he used to receive from Allah. That is why the Holy Quran has held it to be the 'obedience of Allah' Himself. On the other hand, no ruler or a head of a state can claim to receive any revelation of any kind.

It is for this reason that a ruler can enjoy an administrative authority over his subjects, but he cannot lay down the rules of Shari'ah. His orders are purely administrative orders, which are to be obeyed by the citizens in that capacity alone. He cannot override any rule of *Shari'ah* enshrined in the Holy Quran and *sunnah*, nor can his orders be regarded as imperatives for all times to come, as those of Shari'ah, because they are not based on any revelation from Allah. They are effective only in a sphere where the *shari'ah* has not given any definite rule, and left the matter on the discretion of a ruler.

The case of the Holy Prophet ﷺ is totally different. He, as a messenger, receives revelation from Allah, recited and unrecited both. His prophetic orders, therefore, are not just administrative orders based on his personal perception. They are based on the revelation, or, at least, are confirmed by it. Let me now explain both situations:

The orders of the Holy Prophet ﷺ are sometimes based on the revelation in the sense that the revelation 'recited or unrecited' is their original source. But for this revelation, he would not deliver such orders. There can be no doubt in their divine nature. Hence, they form part of the *Shari'ah*.

In some cases, however, the origin of the orders is not a revelation. They are based originally on the Holy Prophet's own analysis of the affairs. But they are confirmed by a revelation later on. This confirmation again is of two kinds: sometimes it occurs in explicit terms, whereby the decision of the Holy Prophet ﷺ is upheld by a revelation, and sometimes it happens to be an implied confirmation. If Allah Almighty does not object to a certain act of the Holy Prophet ﷺ, it necessarily implies that the act has been confirmed by Him.

The reason is obvious. A prophet of Allah, being a spokesman of His pleasure, remains under a constant divine supervision. If he says something or does something, which is not in complete consonance with Allah's pleasure, he is always warned about it. In a number of verses, the Holy Quran has expressed Allah's disapproval of some acts done or intended by the Holy Prophet ﷺ. Thus, no act of the Holy Prophet ﷺ has ever gone unchecked.

In this perspective, if the Holy Prophet ﷺ does some thing or issues an order, and no revelation, recited or unrecited, comes to disapprove the same, it necessarily implies that the act or order has been approved by Allah Almighty, because if the converse were true, the revelation would never remain silent; it would certainly come to correct the error, as it came in certain cases where disapproval was conveyed in direct terms to the Holy Prophet ﷺ.

Thus, whatever he says or does in his capacity of a messenger, and no revelation comes to the contrary, it is deemed to be an implied confirmation of his saying or act.

It is, therefore, true to say that all his orders and acts are either based on the revelation, or confirmed by it, explicitly or implicitly.

No such authority can be attributed to any ruler after him, because the revelation after him came to an end. This is why the Holy Quran highlights the obedience of the messenger as distinct from that of the ruling authorities.

On these three major grounds, there is no room for the misconception that the 'obedience of the Messenger' emphasized by the Holy Quran means the 'obedience of the ruling authority'. In fact, his obedience is necessary for the sole reason that he is a prophet, and his orders and acts, reflect the pleasure of Allah. Hence, the 'Sunnah' which is nothing but a record of his sayings and acts, enjoys a binding authority on all Muslims who believe in Allah and His Holy Book.

CHAPTER 2

The Scope of the Prophetic Authority

The verses of the Quran quoted in the previous chapter, and the natural conclusions derived therefrom, are sufficient to prove the authority of the 'Sunnah' of the Holy Prophet ﷺ. Its being a source of Islamic law stands proved on that score. Yet. the Holy Quran has not only stressed upon the 'obedience of the Messenger' as a general rule or principle; It has also highlighted the different shades of authority in order to explain the scope of his obedience, and the various spheres where it is to be applied.

Therefore, we propose in this chapter to deal with each of these spheres separately, and to explain what the Holy Quran requires of us in respect of each of them.

The Prophet's Authority to make laws

A number of verses in the Holy Quran establish the authority of the Holy Prophet ﷺ as a legislator or a law - maker. Some of those are reproduced below:

وَرَحْمَتِي وَسِعَتْ كُلَّ شَيْءٍ فَسَأَكْتُبُهَا لِلَّذِيْنَ
يَتَّقُوْنَ وَيُؤْتُوْنَ الزَّكَاةَ وَالَّذِيْنَ هُمْ بِآيَاتِنَا
يُؤْمِنُونَ الَّذِيْنَ يَتَّبِعُونَ الرَّسُوْلَ النَّبِيَّ الأُمِّيَّ
الَّذِى يَجِدُوْنَه مَكْتُوْبًا عِنْدَهُمْ فِي التَّوْرَاةِ
وَالإِنْجِيْلِ، يَأْمُرُهُمْ بِالْمَعْرُوْفِ وَيَنْهَاهُمْ عَنِ
الْمُنْكَرِ وَيُحِلُّ لَهُمُ الطَّيِّبَاتِ وَيُحَرِّمُ عَلَيْهِمُ
الْخَبَائِثَ وَيَضَعُ عَنْهُمْ إِصْرَهُمْ وَالأَغْلالَ الَّتِي
كَانَتْ عَلَيْهِمْ، فَالَّذِيْنَ آمَنُوْا بِهِ وَعَزَّرُوْهُ
وَنَصَرُوْهُ وَاتَّبَعُوا النُّوْرَ الَّذِى أُنْزِلَ مَعَهُ أُولَئِكَ
هُمُ الْمُفْلِحُوْنَ. (الأعراف: ١٥٦و١٥٧)

And My mercy embraces all things. So, I shall prescribe it for those who fear Allah, and pay *zakah* (obligatory alms), and those who have faith in Our signs, those who follow the Messenger, the unlettered Prophet whom they find written down in the Torah and the Injil, and who bids them to the Fair and forbids them the Unfair, *and makes lawful for them the good things, and makes unlawful for them the impure things,* and relieves them of their burdens and of the shackles that were upon them. So , those who believe in him, and honour him, and help him, and follow the light that has been sent down with him - they are the ones who acquire success" (7:157)

The italicized words in this verse signify that one of the functions of the Holy Propeht ﷺ, is " to make lawful the good things and make unlawful the impure things. " This function has been separated from 'bidding the Fair and forbidding the Unfair', because the latter relates to the preaching of what has already been established as Fair, and warning against what is established as Unfair, while the former embodies the making of lawful and unlawful, that is, the enforcing of new laws regarding the permissibility or prohibition of things. This function of prescribing new religious laws and rules is attributed here not to the Holy Quran, but to the Holy Prophet ﷺ. It, therefore, cannot be argued that the 'making lawful or unlawful' means the declaration of what is laid down in the Holy Quran only, because the declaration of a law is totally different from making it.

Besides, the declaration of the established rules has been referred to in the earlier sentence separately, that is, 'bids them to the Fair and forbids for them the Unfair. The reference in the next sentence, therefore, is only to 'making' new laws.

The verse also emphasises 'to believe' in the Holy Prophet ﷺ. In the present context, it clearly means to believe in all his functions mentioned in the verse including to make something 'lawful' or 'unlawful'.

The verse, moreover, directs to follow the light that has been sent down with him. Here again, instead of 'following the Holy Quran', 'following the light' has been ordered, so as to include all the imperatives sent down to the Holy Prophet ﷺ, either through the Holy Book or through the unrecited revelation, reflecting in his own orders and acts.

Looked at from whatever angle, this verse is a clear proof of the fact that the Holy Prophet ﷺ had an authority based, of course, on the unrecited revelation, to make new laws in addition to those mentioned in the Holy Quran.

2. The Holy Quran says:

قَاتِلُوا الَّذِيْنَ لَايُؤْمِنُوْنَ بِاللهِ وَ لَابِالْيَوْمِ
الْآخِرِ وَلَايُحَرِّمُوْنَ مَا حَرَّمَ اللهُ وَرَسُوْلُهُ

(التوبة، ۲۹)

> Fight those who do not believe in Allah and the Hereafter and *do not hold unlawful what Allah and His Messenger have made unlawful* (9:29:)

The underlined words signify that it is necessary 'to hold unlawful what Allah and His Messenger made unlawful', and that the authority making something unlawful' is not restricted to Allah Almighty. The Holy Prophet ﷺ can also, by the will of Allah, exercise this authority. The difference between the authority of Allah and that of the Messenger is, no doubt, significant. The former is wholly independent, intrinsic and self-existent, while the authority of the latter is derived from and dependent on the revelation from Allah. Yet, the fact remains that the Holy Prophet ﷺ has this authority and it is necessary for believers to submit to it alongwith their submission to the authority of Allah.

3. The Holy Quran says,

وَمَا كَانَ لِمُؤْمِنٍ وَلَامُؤْمِنَةٍ إِذَا قَضَى اللهُ
وَرَسُوْلُهُ أَمْرًا أَنْ يَكُوْنَ لَهُمُ الْخِيَرَةُ مِنْ أَمْرِهِمْ
وَمَنْ يَّعْصِ اللَّهَ وَرَسُوْلَهُ فَقَدْ ضَلَّ ضَلَالًا
مُّبِيْنًا (الأحزاب، ٣٦)

> No believer, neither man nor woman, has a right, when Allah and His Messenger decide a matter, to have a choice in their matter in issue. And whoever disobeys Allah and His Messenger has gone astray into manifest error. (33:36)

Here, the decisions of Allah and the Messenger ﷺ both have been declared binding on the believers.

It is worth mentioning that the word 'and' occuring between 'Allah' and 'His Messenger' carries both conjunctive and disjunctive meanings. It cannot be held to give conjunctive sense only, because in that case it will exclude the decision of Allah unless it is combined with the decision of the messenger - a construction too fallacious to be imagined in the divine expression.

The only reasonable construction, therefore, is to take the word 'and' in both conjunctive and disjunctive meanings. The sense is that whenever Allah or His Messenger, any one or both of them, decide a matter, the believers have no choice except to submit to their decision.

It is thus clear that the Holy Prophet ﷺ has the legal authority to deliver decisions in the collective and individual affairs of the believers who are bound to surrender to those decisions

4. The Holy Quran says,

مَا آتَاكُمُ الرَّسُولُ فَخُذُوهُ وَمَانَهَاكُمْ عَنْهُ فَانْتَهُوا (الحشر : ٧)

Whatever the Messenger gives you, take it, and whatever he forbids you, refrain from it (59:7)

Although the context of this verse relates to the distribution of the spoils of war, yet it is the well known principle of the interpretation of the Holy Quran that, notwithstanding the particular event in which a verse is revealed, if the words used are general, they are to be construed in their general sense; they cannot be restricted to that particular event.

Keeping in view this principle, which is never disputed, the verse gives a general rule about the Holy Prophet ﷺ that whatever order he gives is binding on the believers and, whatever thing he forbids stands prohibited for them. The Holy Quran thus has conferred a legal authority to the Holy Prophet ﷺ to give orders, to make laws and to enforce prohibitions.

It will be interesting here to cite a wise answer of Abdullah ibn Mas'ud, the blessed companion of the Holy Prophet ﷺ

which he gave to a woman.

A woman from the tribe of Asad came to Abdullah b. Mas'ud and said, ' I have come to know that you hold such and such things as prohibited. I have gone through the whole Book of Allah, but never found any such probibition in it'.

Abdullah b. Mas'ud replied, "Had you read the Book, you would have found it. Allah Almighty says :*

> Whatever the Messenger gives you, take it, and whatever he forbids you, refrain from it." (59: 7)

By this answer Abdullah b. Mas'ud pointed out that this verse is so comprehensive that it embodies all the orders and prohibitions of the Holy Prophet ﷺ and since the questioned prohibitions are enforced by the Holy Prophet ﷺ they form part of this verse, though indirectly.

5. The Holy Quran says.

فَلَاوَرَبِّكَ لَايُؤْمِنُونَ حَتَّى يُحَكِّمُوكَ فِيمَا
شَجَرَ بَيْنَهُمْ ثُمَّ لَايَجِدُوْا فِي أَنْفُسِهِمْ حَرَجًا مِمَّا
قَضَيْتَ وَيُسَلِّمُوْا تَسْلِيمًا (النساء : ٦٥)

> But no, by your Lord, they shall not be (deemed to be) believers unless they accept you as judge in their disputes, then find in their hearts no adverse feeling against what you decided, but serrender to it in complete submission (4:65)

The authority of the Holy Prophet ﷺ established in this verse seems apparantly to be an authority to adjudicate in the disputes brought before him. But after due consideration in the

---

* Reported by Ibn Majah V.1. Ch.10:52P.367 Hadith 1998

construction used here, this authority appears to be more than that of a judge. A judge, no doubt, has an authority to deliver his judgments and the parties concerned are bound to obey his judgments, but the submission to his judgments is not a condition for being a Muslim. If somebody does not accept the judgment of a duly authorised judge, it can be a gross misconduct on his part, and a great sin, for which he may be punished, but he cannot be excluded from the pale of Islam on this score alone. He cannot be held as disbeliever.

On the contrary, the verse vehemently insists that the person who does not accept the verdicts of the Holy Prophet ﷺ cannot be held to be a believer. This forceful assertion indicates that the authority of the Holy Prophet ﷺ is not merely that of a customary judge. The denial of his judgments amounts to disbelief. It implies that the verdicts of the Holy Prophet ﷺ referred to here are not the normal verdicts given in the process of a trial. They are the laws laid down by him on the basis of the revelation, recited or unrecited, that he receives from Allah. So, the denial of these laws is, in fact, the denial of the divine orders which excludes the denier from the pale of Islam.

Looked at from this point of view, this verse gives the Holy Prophet ﷺ not only the authority of a judge, but also confers upon him the authority to make laws, as binding on the Muslims as the divine laws .

6. The Holy Quran says:

وَيَقُولُونَ آمَنَّا بِاللهِ وَبِالرَّسُولِ وَأَطَعْنَا ثُمَّ
يَتَوَلَّى فَرِيقٌ مِّنْهُم مِّنْ بَعْدِ ذَلِكَ وَمَا أُولَئِكَ
بِالْمُؤْمِنِينَ وَإِذَا دُعُوا إِلَى اللهِ وَرَسُولِهِ لِيَحْكُمَ
بَيْنَهُمْ إِذَا فَرِيقٌ مِّنْهُم مُّعْرِضُونَ. وَإِن يَكُن لَّهُمُ
الْحَقُّ يَأْتُوا إِلَيْهِ مُذْعِنِينَ أَفِي قُلُوبِهِم مَّرَضٌ أَم

ارتابوا أم يخافوا أن يَحِيفَ اللّهُ عَلَيْهِمْ
وَرَسُولُهُ بَلْ أولئِكَ هُمُ الظَّالِمُوْنَ إِنَّمَا كَانَ قَوْلَ
الْمُؤْمِنِيْنَ إِذَا دُعُوا إِلَى اللهِ وَرَسُوْلِهِ لِيَحْكُمَ
بَيْنَهُمْ أن يَقُولُوْا سَمِعْنَا وَأَطَعْنَا وَأولئِكَ هُمُ
الْمُفْلِحُوْنَ وَمَن يُطِعِ اللهَ وَرَسُولَهُ وَيَخْشَ اللهَ
وَيَتَّقْهِ فَأولئِكَ هُمُ الْفَائِزُوْنَ (النور: ٤٧-٥١)

They say, 'we believe in Allah and the Messenger, and we obey.' Then, after that, a group of them turn away. And they are not believers. And when they are called to Allah and His Messenger that he may judge between them, suddenly a group of them turn back. But if they had a right, they come to him submissively! Is it that there is sickness in their hearts? Or are they in doubt? Or do they fear that Allah may be unjust towards them, and His Messenger? Nay, but *they* are the unjust. All that the believers say when they are called to Allah and His Messenger that he (the Messenger) may judge between them, is that they say, 'We hear and we obey.' And they are those who acquire success. And whoever obeys Allah and His Messenger and fears Allah and observes His Awe, such are those who are the winners." (24:47-52)

These verses, too, hold that, in order to be a Muslim, the condition is to surrender to the verdicts of the Holy Prophet ﷺ. Those who do not turn towards him in their disputes inspite of being called to him cannot, according to the Holy Quran, be treated as believers. It carries the same principle as mentioned in the preceding verse: It is the basic ingredient of the belief in Allah and His Messenger that the authority of the Messenger should be accepted whole- heartedly. He must be consulted in disputes and obeyed. His verdicts must be followed in total submission, and the laws enunciated by him must be held as binding.

The Holy Prophet's Authority to Interpret the Holy Quran.

The second type of authority given to the Holy Prophet ﷺ is the authority to interpret and explain the Holy Book. He is the final authority in the interpretation of the Holy Quran. The Holy Quran says:

وَأَنزَلْنَا إِلَيْكَ الذِّكْرَ لِتُبَيِّنَ لِلنَّاسِ مَا نُزِّلَ
إِلَيْهِمْ وَلَعَلَّهُمْ يَتَفَكَّرُونَ (النحل: ٤٤)

> And We sent down towards you the Advice * (i.e. the Quran) so that you may explain to the people what has been sent down to them and, so that they may ponder (16:44).

It is unequivocally established here that the basic function of the Holy Prophet ﷺ is to explain the Holy Book and to interpret the revelation sent down to him. It is obvious that the Arabs of Makkah, who were directly addressed by the Holy Prophet ﷺ did not need any translation of the Quranic text. The Holy Quran was revealed in their own mother tongue. Despite that they were mostly illiterate, they had a command on their language and literature. Their beautiful poetry, their eloquent speeches and their impressive dialogues are the basic sources of

---

* The original Arabic word is dhikr which refers here undisputedly to the Holy Quran.

richness in the Arabic literature. They needed no one to teach them the literal meaning of the Quranic text. That they understood the textual meaning is beyond any doubt.

It is thus obvious that the explanation entrusted to the Holy Prophet ﷺ was something more than the literal meaning of the Book. It was an explanation of what Allah Almighty intended, including all the implications involved and the details needed. These details are also received by the Holy Prophet ﷺ through the unrecited revelation. As discussed earlier, the Holy Quran has clearly said.

ثم إنَّ علينا بيانه (القيامة : ١٩)

Then, it is on Us to explain it (75:19)

This verse is self-explanatory on the subject. Allah Almighty has Himself assured the Holy Prophet ﷺ that He shall explain the Book to him. So, whatever explanation the Holy Prophet gives to the Book is based on the explanation of Allah Himself. So, his interpretion of the Holy Quran overrides all the possible interpretations Hence, he is the final authority in the exegesis and interpretation. of the Holy Quran. His word is the last word in this behalf.

Examples of Prophetic explanations of the Quran

To be more specific, I would give a few concrete instances of the explanations of the Holy Book given to us by the Holy Prophet ﷺ. These examples will also show the drastic amount of what we lose if we ignore the *Sunnah* of the Holy Prophet ﷺ :

1. The *salah* (prayer) is the well-known way of worship

which is undisputedly held as the first pillar of Islam after having faith. The Holy Quran has ordered more than 73 times to observe it. Despite this large number of verses giving direct command to observe the *Salah*, there is no verse in the entire Book to explain how to perform and observe it.

Some components of the *salah*, like *ruku'* (bowing down) or *sujud* (Prostration) or *Qiyam* (standing) are, no doubt, mentioned in the Holy Quran. But the complete way to perform *salah* as a composite whole has never been explained. It is only through the *Sunnah* of the Holy Prophet ﷺ that we learn the exact way to perfom it. If the *Sunnah* is ignored, all these details about the correct way of observing *salah* are totally lost. Not only this, nobody can bring forth an alternate way to perform *salah* on the basis of the Holy Quran alone.

It is significant that the Holy Quran has repeated the command of observing *salah* as many as 73 times, yet, it has elected not to describe the way it had to be performed. This is not without some wisdom behind it. The point that seems to have been made delibrately is one of the significance of the *Sunnah*.

By avoiding the details about no less a pillar of Islam than *salah*, it is pointed out that the Holy Quran is meant for giving the fundamental principles only. The details are left to the explanations of the Holy Prophet ﷺ .

2. Moreover, it is mentioned in the Holy Quran that the '*salah*' is tied up with some prescribed times. Allah Almighty says:

إِنَّ الصَّلَاةَ كَانَتْ عَلَى الْمُؤْمِنِيْنَ كِتَابًا مَّوْقُوْتًا (النساء : ١٠٤)

Surely, the *salah* is a timed obligation for the believers(4:104)

It is clear from this verse that there are some particular times in which the *salah* should be performed. But what are those times is nowhere mentioned in the Holy Quran. Even that the daily obligatory prayers are five in number is never disclosed in the Holy Book. It is only through the *Sunnah* of the Holy Prophet ﷺ that we have learnt the exact number and the specific times of the obligatory prayers.

3. The same is the position of the number of *Rak'at* to be performed in each prayer. It is not mentioned anywhere in the Holy Quran that the number of *Rak'at* is two in Fajr, four in Zuhr, Asr and Isha; it is only in the *Sunnah* that these matters are mentioned.

If the *Sunnah* is not believed, all these necessary details even about the first pillar of Islam remain totally unknown, so as to render the *salah* too vague an obligation to be carried out in practice.

4. The same is the case of *Zakah* (alms giving), the second pillar of Islam, which is in most cases combined with the *Salah* in the Holy Quran. The order to 'pay *zakah*' is found in the Holy Book in more than thirty places. But who is liable to pay it ? On what rate it should be paid? What assets are liable to the obligation of Zakah? What assets are exempted from it? All these questions remain unanswered if the *Sunnah* of the Holy Prophet ﷺ is ignored. It is the Holy Prophet ﷺ who explained all these details about zakah.

5. Fasts of Ramadan are held to be the third pillar of Islam. Here again only the fundamental principles are found in the Holy Quran. Most of the necessary details have been left to the explanation of the Holy Prophet ﷺ which he disclosed through his sayings and acts. What acts, other than eating, drinking and having sex, are prohibited or permitted during the fast? Under what conditions can one break the fast during the day? What kind of treatment can be undertaken in the state of fasting? All these and similar other details are mentioned by the Holy Prophet ﷺ .

6. The Holy Quran has said after mentioning how to perform *wudu*, (ablution):

وَإِنْ كُنْتُمْ جُنُبًا فَاطَّهَّرُوْا (المائدة ٦:)

And if you are *junub* (defiled) well-purify yourself (5:6)

It is also clarified in the Holy Quran that while being *junub* (defiled) one should not perform prayers (4:43). But the definition of *junub* (defiled) is nowhere given in the Holy Quran nor is it mentioned how should a defiled person 'well-purify' himself. It is the Holy Prophet ﷺ who has explained all these questions and laid down the detailed injunctions on the subject.

7. The command of the Holy Quran concerning Hajj, the fourth pillar of Islam, is in the following words:

وَلِلّٰهِ عَلَى النَّاسِ حِجُّ الْبَيْتِ مَنِ اسْتَطَاعَ
إِلَيْهِ سَبِيْلاً (آل عمران : ٩٧)

And as a right of Allah, it is obligatory on people to perform the Hajj of the House - whoever has the ability to manage his way to it. (3 : 97)

It is just not disclosed here as to how many times the Hajj (pilgrimage to Makkah) is obligatory? The Holy Prophet ﷺ explained that the obligation is discharged by performing Hajj only once in a life-time.

8. The Holy Quran says:

اَلَّذِيْنَ يَكْنِزُوْنَ الذَّهَبَ وَالْفِضَّةَ وَلَايُنْفِقُوْنَهَا
فِي سَبِيْلِ اللهِ فَبَشِّرْهُمْ بِعَذَابٍ اَلِيْمٍ

Those who accumulate gold and silver and do not spend them in the way of Allah, give them the good news of a painful punishment (9:34)

Here, 'accumulation' is prohibited and 'spending' is enjoined. But the quantum of none of the two is explained. Upto what limit can one save his money, and how much spending is obligatory? Both the questions are left to the explanation of the Holy Prophet ﷺ who has laid down the detailed rules in this respect.

9. The Holy Quran, while describing the list of the women of prohibited degree, with whom one cannot marry, has extended the prohibition to marrying two sisters in one time:

وَأَنْ تَجْمَعُوا بَيْنَ الأُخْتَيْنِ (النساء : ٢٣)

And (it is also prohibited) to combine two sisters together (4:23)

The Holy Prophet ﷺ while explaining this verse, clarified that the prohibition is not restricted to two sisters only. The verse has, instead, laid down a principle which includes the prohibition of combining an aunt and her niece, paternal or maternal, as well.

10. The Holy Quran says:

اَلْيَوْمَ أُحِلَّ لَكُمُ الطَّيِّبَاتِ (المائدة : ٥)

Today the good things have been permitted to you. (5:5)

Here 'the good things' are not explained. The detailed list of the lawful 'good things' has only been given by the Holy Prophet ﷺ who has described the different kinds of food being not lawful for the Muslims and not falling in the category of 'good things'. Had there been no such explanation given by the Holy Prophet ﷺ everybody could interpret the 'good things' according to his own personal desires, and the very purpose of the revelation, namely, to draw a clear distinction between good and bad, could have been disturbed. If everybody was free to determine what is good and what is bad, neither any revelation nor a messenger was called for. It was through both the Holy Book and the Messenger ﷺ that the need was fulfilled.

Numerous other examples of this nature may be cited. But the few examples given above are, perhaps, quite sufficient to show the nature of the explanations given by the Holy Prophet ﷺ as well as to establish their necessity in the framework of an Islamic life ordained by the Holy Quran for its followers.

Does the Holy Quran need explanation?

Before concluding this descussion, it is pertinent to answer a question often raised with reference to the explanation of the Holy Quran. The question is whether the Holy Quran needs any one to explain its contents? The Holy Quran in certain places seems to claim that its verses are self explanatory, easy to understand and clear in their meanings. So, any external explanation should be uncalled for. Why, then, the prophetic explanation is so much stressed upon?

The answer to this question is found in the Holy Quran itself. A combined study of the relevant verses reveals that the Holy Quran deals with two different types of subjects. One is concerned with the general statements about the simple realities, and it includes the historic events relating to the former prophets and their nations, the statement of Allah's bounties on mankind, the creation of the heavens and the earth, the cosmological signs of the divine power and wisdom, the pleasures of the Paradise and the torture of the Hell, and subjects of similar nature.

The other type of subjects consists of the imperatives of *Shari'ah*, the provisions of Islamic law, the details of doctrinal issues, the wisdom of certain injunctions, and other academic subjects.

The first type of subject, which is termed in the Holy Quran as *Zikr* (the lesson, the sermon, the advice) is, no doubt, so easy to understand that even an illiterate rustic can benefit from it without having recourse to anyone else. It is in this type of subjects that the Holy Quran says:

وَلَقَدْ يَسَّرْنَا الْقُرآنَ لِلذِّكْرِ فَهَلْ مِن مُّدَّكِرٍ

(القمر، ٢٢)

And surely we have made the Quran easy for *Zikr* (getting a lesson) so, is there anyone to get a lesson?(54:22)

The words 'for *Zikr*' (getting a lesson) signify that the easiness of the Holy Quran relates to the subjects of the first nature. The basic thrust of the verse is on getting lesson from the Quran and its being easy for this purpose only. But by no means the proposition can be extended to the inference of legal rules and the interpretation of the legal and doctrinal provisions contained in the Book. Had the interpretation of even this type of subjects been open to everybody irrespective of the volume of his learning, the Holy Quran would have not entrusted the Holy Prophet ﷺ with the functions of 'teaching' and 'explaining' the Book. The verses qouted earlier, which introduce the Holy Prophet ﷺ as the one who 'teaches' and 'explains' the Holy Quran, are explicit on the point that the Book needs some messenger to teach and interpret it. Regarding the type of verses which require explanation, the Holy Quran itself says,

وَتِلْكَ الأَمْثَالُ نَضْرِبُهَا لِلنَّاسِ وَمَايَعْقِلُهَا إِلاَّ الْعَالِمُوْنَ (العنكبوت: ٤٣)

And these similitudes We mention before the people. And nobody understands them except the learned. (29:43)

Thus, the 'easiness' of the subjects of the first type does not exclude the necessity of a prophet who can explain all the legal and practical implications of the imperatives contained in the Holy Quran.

The Time Limit of the Prophetic authority

We have so far studied the two types of the Prophetic authority, first being the authority to make new laws in addition to those contained in the Holy Quran, and the second being the authority to explain, interpret and expound the Quranic injunctions.

But before proceeding to other aspects of the Prophetic authority, another issue should be resolved just here.

It is sometimes argued by those who hesitate to accept the full authority of the Sunnah, that whenever the Holy Quran has conferred on the Holy Prophet an authority to make laws or to explain and interpret the Book, it meant this authority to be binding on the people of the Prophet 's time only. They were under the direct control and the instant supervision of the Holy Prophet ﷺ and were addressed by him face to face. Therefore, the Prophetic authority was limited to them only. It cannot be extended to all the generations for all times to come.

This contention leads us to the discovery of the time limits of the Prophetic authority. The question is whether the authority of the Holy Prophet ﷺ was confined to his own time, or it is an everlasting authority which holds good for all times to come.

The basic question underlying this issue has already been answered in detail; and that is the question of the nature of this authority. It has been established through a number of arguments that the obedience of the Holy Prophet ﷺ was not enjoined upon the Muslims in his capacity of a ruler. It has been enjoined in his capacity of a prophet . Had it been the authority of a ruler only, which the Holy Prophet ﷺ exercised, it would logically be inferred that the authority is tied up with his rule, and as soon as his administrative rule is over, his authority simultaneously ceases to have effect.

But if the authority is a 'Prophetic' authority, and not merely a 'ruling authority', then, it is obvious that it shall continue with the continuance of the prophethood, and shall not disappear until the Holy Prophet ﷺ no longer remains a Prolphet.

Now, the only question is whether the Holy Prophet ﷺ was a prophet of a particular nation or a particular time, or his prophethood extended to the whole mankind for all times. Let us seek the answer from the Holy Quran itself. The Holy Quran says:

قُلْ يَا أَيُّهَا النَّاسُ إِنِّى رَسُوْلُ اللهِ إِلَيْكُمْ
جَمِيْعًا (الأعراف: ١٥٨)

Say, 'O mankind, I am the Messenger of Allah to you all' (7:158)

وَمَاأَرْسَلْنَاكَ إِلاَّ كَافَّةً لِلنَّاسِ بَشِيْراً وَّنَذِيْراً

(السبا، ٢٨)

And We did not send you (O Prophet) except to the entire mankind, bearing good news, and warning. (34:28)

وَمَا أَرْسَلْنٰكَ إِلاَّ رَحْمَةً لِّلعَالَمِيْنَ

(الأنبياء، ٢١)

And We did not send you, save as a mercy unto all the worlds. (21:107)

تَبَارَكَ الَّذِى نَزَّلَ الفُرْقَانَ عَلَى عَبْدِهِ
لِيَكُوْنَ لِلعَالَمِيْنَ نَذِيْراً (الفرقان: ١)

Blessed be He Who has sent down the Quran on His servant so that he may be a warner to all the worlds. (25:1)

وَأَرْسَلْنَاكَ لِلنَّاسِ رَسُوْلاً وَكَفَى بِاللهِ شَهِيْدًا

(النساء : ٨٩)

And We have sent you (O Prophet,) for mankind as a Messenger. And Allah suffices to be a witness (4:79).

And the whole mankind is addressed when it is said:

يَا أَيُّهَا النَّاسُ قَدْ جَاءَكُمُ الرَّسُوْلُ بِالْحَقِّ
مِنْ رَّبِّكُمْ فَآمِنُوْا خَيْرًا لَّكُمْ وَإِنْ تَكْفُرُوْا فَإِنَّ
لِلَّهِ مَا فِي السَّمٰوَاتِ وَالأَرْضِ وَكَانَ اللّٰهُ عَلِيْمًا
حَكِيْمًا . (النساء : ١٧٠)

O mankind, the Messenger has come to you with the truth from your Lord, so believe; it is better for you. And if you disbelieve, to Allah belongs what is in the heavens and in the earth. And Allah is All - Knowing, All-Wise (4:170).

The first five verses need no elaboration. They are self-explanatory on the point that the Holy Prophet ﷺ was sent to the whole mankind and not to a particular people; his prophethood was not limited either in time or in place.

The fifth verse addresses the whole mankind and enjoins upon all of them to believe in the Holy Prophet ﷺ . Nobody can say that the belief of the Holy Prophet ﷺ was restricted to his own time. It is, according to this verse, incumbent upon all the peoples, of whatever age, to believe in his Prophethood.

It is also mentioned in the Holy Quran that the Holy

Prophet ﷺ is the last Messenger after whom no Prophet is to come:

ما كان محمد أبا أحد من رجالكم ولكن رسول
الله وخاتم النبيين وكان الله على كل شئ قديرا

Muhammad is not the father of anyone of your men, but the Messenger of Allah and the last of the prophets. And Allah is All-Knowing in respect of everything (33:40).

This verse made it clear that the Holy Prophet ﷺ is the last one in the chain of prophets. The earlier prophets were often sent to a particular nation for a particular time, because they were succeeded by other prophets. But no prophet is to come after Muhammad ﷺ . Hence, his prophethood extends to all the nations and all the times. This is what the Holy Prophet ﷺ himself explained in the following words:

كا نت بنو إسرائيل تسوسهم الأنبياء ،
كلما هلك نبيّ خلفه نبيّ، وإنه لانبيّ بعدى،
وسيكون خلفاء فيكثرون

"The Israelites were led by the prophets. Whenever a prophet would pass away, another prophet would succeed him. But there is no prophet after me. However, there shall be successors, and shall be in large numbers.*

If the realm of his prophethood would not reach out to the next generations, the people of those generations would be left devoid of the prophetic guidance, while Allah does not leave any people without prophetic guidance.

---

* Sahih al Bukhari, Ch. 50 Anbiya, Hadeeth 3455.

In the light of the verses quoted above, there remains no doubt in the fact that the Holy Prophet ﷺ is a messenger to all the nations for all times to come.

If his prophethood extends to all times, there remains no room for the suggestion that his prophetic authority does no longer hold good , and the present day Muslims are not bound to obey and follow him.

There is another point in the subject worth attention:

It is established through a large number of arguments in the first chapter that Allah Almighty sent no divine book without a messenger. It is also clarified by Allah that the messengers are sent to teach the Book and to explain it. It is also proved earlier that, but for the detailed explanations of the Holy Prophet, nobody might know even the way of obligatory prayers.

The question now is whether all these Prophetic explanations were needed only by the Arabs of the Prophetic age. The Arabs of Makkah were more aware of the Arabic language than we are. They were more familiar to the Quranic style. They were physically present at the time of revelation and observed personally all the surrounding circumstances in which the Holy Book was revealed. They received the verses of the Holy Quran from the mouth of the Holy Prophet ﷺ, and were fully aware of all the factors which help in the correct understanding of a text. Still, they needed the explanations of the Holy Prophet ﷺ which were binding on them.

Then, how can a man of ordinary perception presume that the people of this age, who lack all these advantages, do not need the explanations of a prophet? We have neither that command on the Arabic language as they had, nor are we so familiar with the

Quranic style as they were, nor have we seen the circumstances in which the Holy Quran was revealed, as they have seen. If they needed the guidance of the Holy Prophet ﷺ in interpretting the Holy Quran, we should certainly need it all the more.

If the authority of the Holy Quran has no time-limit, if the text of the Quran is binding on all the generations for all times to come, then, the authority of the Messenger which is included in the very Quran without being limited to any time bond, shall remain as effective as the Holy Quran itself. While ordaining for the 'obedience of the messengers 'the Holy Quran addressed not only the Arabs of Makkah or Madinah. It has addressed all the believers when it was said:

يَا أَيُّهَا الَّذِيْنَ آمَنُوْا أَطِيْعُوا اللّٰهَ وَأَطِيْعُوا الرَّسُوْلَ

O those who believe, obey Allah and obey the Messenger (4:59)

If the 'obedience of Allah' has always been combined with the 'obedience of the Messenger' as we have seen earlier, there is no room for separating any one from the other. If one is meant for all times, the other cannot be meant for a particular period. The Holy Quran at another place has also warned against such separation between Allah and His Messenger:

إِنَّ الَّذِيْنَ يَكْفُرُوْنَ بِاللهِ وَرُسُلِهِ وَيُرِيْدُوْنَ أَنْ يُفَرِّقُوا بَيْنَ اللهِ وَرُسُلِهِ وَيَقُوْلُوْنَ نُؤْمِنُ بِبَعْضٍ وَّ نَكْفُرُ بِبَعْضٍ وَّيُرِيْدُوْنَ أَنْ يَّتَّخِذُوا بَيْنَ ذٰلِكَ سَبِيْلاً أُولٰئِكَ هُمُ الْكَافِرُوْنَ حَقًّا وَأَعْتَدْنَا لِلْكَافِرِيْنَ عَذَابًا مُّهِيْنًا

(النساء، ١٥١,١٥٠)

> Those who disbelieve in Allah and His Messengers, and desire to make separation between Allah and His messengers, and say, 'we believe in some, and disbelieve in some' desiring to adopt a way in between this and that-- those are the unbelievers in truth, and We have prepared for the desbelievers a humiliating punishment (4:150,151)

Therefore, the submission to the authority of the Holy Prophet ﷺ is a basic ingredient of having belief in his prophethood, which can never be separated from him. Thus, to accept the prophetic authority in the early days of Islam, and to deny it in the later days, is so fallacious a proposition that cannot find support from any source of Islamic learning, nor can it be accepted on any touchstone of logic and reason.

The Prophetic Authority in Worldly Affairs

Another point of view often presented by some westernised circles is that the authority of the Holy Prophet ﷺ is, no doubt, established by the Holy Quran even for all the generations for all times to come. But the scope of this authority is limited only to the doctrinal affairs and the matters of worship. The function of a prophet, according to them, is restricted to correct the doctrinal beliefs of the *ummah* and to teach them how to worship Allah. As far as the worldly affairs are concerned, they are not governed by the prophetic authority. These worldly affairs include, in their view, all the economic, social and political affairs which should be settled according to the expediency at each relevant time, and the Prophetic authority has no concern with them. Even if the Holy Prophet gives some directions in these fields, he does so in his private capacity, and not as a Messenger. So, it is not necessary for the *Ummah* to comply with such directions.

To substantiate this proposition, a particular tradition of the Holy Prophet ﷺ is often quoted, though out of context, * in which he said to his companions.

أنتم أعلم بأمور دنياكم

You know more about your worldly affairs.

Before I quote this tradition in its full context, the very concept upon which this proposition is based needs examination.

In fact, this view is based on a serious misconception about the whole structure of Islamic order.

The misconception is that Islam, like some other religions, is restricted only to some doctrines and some rituals. It has no concern with the day-to-day affairs of the human life. After observing the prescribed doctrines and rituals, everybody is free to run his life in whatever way he likes, not hindered in any manner by the divine imperatives. That is why the advocates of this view confine the Prophetic authority to some doctrines and rituals only.

But the misconception, however fashionable it may seem to be, is a misconception. It is an established fact that Islam, unlike some other religions which can coincide and co-exist with the secular concept of life, is not merely a set of doctrines and rituals. It is a complete way of life which deals with the political, economic and social problems as well as with theological issues. The Holy Quran says,

يَاأَيُّهَا الَّذِيْنَ آمَنُوْا اسْتَجِيْبُوا لِلّٰهِ وَلِلرَّسُوْل

إِذَا دَعَاكُمْ لِمَا يُحْيِيْكُمْ (الأنفال : ٢٤)

---

* The full context of the tradition is coming shortly.

O those who believe, respond to the call of Allah and His Messenger when he calls you for what gives you life (8:24) .

It means that Allah and His Messenger call people towards life. How is it imagined that the affairs of life are totally out of the jurisdiction of Allah and His Messenger? Nobody who has studied the Holy Quran can endorse that its teachings are limited to worship and rituals. There are specific injunctions in the Holy Quran about sale, purchase loans, mortgage, partnership, penal laws, inheritance, matrimonial relations, political affairs, problems of war and peace and other aspects of international relations. If the Islamic teachings were limited to the doctrinal and ritual matters, there is no reason why such injunctions are mentioned in the Holy Quran.

Likewise the *Sunnah* of the Holy Prophet ﷺ deals with the economic, social, political and legal problems in such detail that voluminous books have been written to compile them. How can it be envisaged that the Holy Prophet ﷺ entered this field in such detailed manner without having any authority or jurisdiction?. The injunctions of the Holy Quran and *Sunnah* in this field are so absolute, imperative, and of mandatory nature that they cannot be imagined to be personal advices lacking any legal force.

We have already quoted a large number of verses from the Holy Quran which enjoin the obedience of Allah and the Messenger upon the believers. This 'obedience' has nowhere been limited to some particular field. It is an all-embracing obedience which requires total submission from the believers, having no exception whatsoever.

It is true that in this field, which is termed in the Islamic law as *'mu'amalat'* , the Holy Quran and *Sunnah* have mostly given some broad principles, and left most of the details open to be settled according to ever-changing needs, but in strict conformity with the principles laid down by them. Thus the field not occupied by the Quran and *Sunnah* is a wider field where the requirements of expediency can well play their role. But it does not mean that the Quran and *Sunnah* have no concern with this vital branch of human life which has always been the basic cause of unrest in the history of humanity, and m which the so called 'rational views' mostly conflicting with each other, have always fallen prey to satanic desires leading the world to disaster.

Anyhow, the fallacy of this narrow viewpoint about Islam which excludes all the practical spheres of life from its pale, rather, to be more correct, makes them devoid of its guidance, cannot sustain before the overwhelming arguments which stand to rule it out totally.

The event of fecundation of the palm-trees.

Let me now turn to the tradition which is often quoted to support this fallacious view. The details of the tradition are as follows:

The Arabs of Madinah used to fecundate their palm-trees in order to make them more fruitful. This operation was called *Ta'bir* which is explained by E.W. Lane as below:

> "He fecundated a palm-tree by means of the spadix of the male tree, which is bruised, or brayed, and sprinkled upon the spadix of the female; or by inserting a stalk of a raceme of the male tree into the spathe of the female, after shaking off the pollen of the former upon the spadix of the female" *

* Lane, E.W. Arabic. English exicon.

Keeping this in view, read the following tradition, as mentioned by Imam Muslim in his Sahih: *

عن موسى بن طلحة، عن أبيه، قال:
مررت مع رسول الله صلى الله عليه وسلم
بقوم على رؤوس النخل، فقال: ما يصنع
هؤلاء؟ فقالوا: يلحقونه، يجعلون الذكر في
الأنثى، فتلقح، فقال رسول الله صلى الله عليه
وسلم: ما أظنّ يغني ذلك شيئا- قال: فأخبروا
بذلك، فتركوه، فأخبر بذلك، فتركوه، فأخبر
رسول الله صلى الله عليه وسلم بذلك، فقال:
إن كان ينفعهم ذلك فليصنعوه، فإنّي إنّما
ظننت ظنّا، فلاتؤاخذوني بالظن. ولكن إذا
حدثتكم عن الله شيئا فخذوه به، فإنّي لن
أكذب على الله عزّ وجلّ.

The blessed Companion Talha says:

'I passed alongwith the Holy Prophet ﷺ accross some people who were on the tops of the palm-trees. The Holy Prophet ﷺ asked, 'What are they doing?

Some people said, 'They are fecundating the tree. They insert the male into the female and the tree stands fecundated'. The Holy Prophet ﷺ said, ' I do not think it will be of any use ' The people (who

---

* Sahih of Muslim, 2 P. 264, Kitabul Fazail.

were fecundating the trees) were informed about what the Holy Prophet ﷺ said. So, they stopped this operation. Then the Holy Prophet ﷺ was informed about their withdrawal. On this, the Holy Prophet ﷺ said, 'If it is in fact useful for them, let them do it, because I had only made a guess. So, do not cling to me in my guess. But when I tell you something on behalf of Allah, take it firm, because I shall never tell a lie on behalf of Allah."

According to the blessed Companion Anas , the Holy Prophet ﷺ has also said on this ocassion.

أنتم أعلم بأمور دنياكم

You know more about your worldly affairs.

The words of this tradition, when looked at in its full context, would clearly reveal that the Holy Prophet ﷺ in this case did not deliver an absolute prohibition against the fecundation of the palm trees. There was no question of its being lawful or unlawful. What the Holy Prophet ﷺ did was neither a command, nor a legal or religious prohibition , nor a moral condemnation. It was not even a serious observation. It was only a remark passed by him by the way in the form of an instant and general guess, as he himself clarified later. 'I do not think it will be of any use'. Nobody can take this sentence as a legal or religious observation. That is why the Holy Prophet ﷺ did not address with it the persons involved in the operation, nor did he order to convey his message to them. It was through some other persons that they learned about the remark of the Holy Prophet ﷺ

Although the remark was not in the form of an imperative, but the blessed companions of the Holy Prophet ﷺ used to obey and follow him in everything, not only on the basis of his legal or religious authority, but also out of their profound love towards him. They, therefore, gave up the operation altogether. When the Holy Prophet ﷺ came to know about their having abstained from the operation on the basis of what he remarked, he clarified the position to avoid any misunderstanding.

The substance of his clarification is that only the absolute statements of the Holy Prophet ﷺ are binding, because they are given in his capacity of a prophet on behalf of Allah Almighty. As for a word spoken by him as a personal guess, and not as an absolute statement, it should be duly honoured, but it should not be taken as a part of *Shariah*.

As I have mentioned earlier, there is a vast field in the day-to-day worldly affairs which is not occupied by the *Shariah*, where the people have been allowed to proceed according to their needs and expedience and on the basis of their knowledge and experience. What instruments should be used to fertilise a barren land? How the plants should be nourished? What weapons are more useful for the purpose of defence? What kind of horses are more suitable to ride? What medicine is useful in a certain disease? The questions of this type relate to the field where the *Shari,ah* has not supplied any particular answer. All these and similar other matters are left to the human curiosity which can solve these problems through its efforts.

It is this unoccupied field of *mubahat* about which the Holy Prophet ﷺ observed:

أنتم أعلم بأمور دنياكم

You know best about your worldly affairs.

But it does not include those worldly affairs in which the Holy Quran or the Sunnah have laid down some specific rules or given a positive command. That is why the Holy Prophet ﷺ, while declaring the matter of the palm-trees to be in the unoccupied field, has simultaneously observed, "But when I tell you something on behalf of Allah, take it firm."

The upshot of the foregoing discussion is that the *Sunnah*

of the Holy Prophet ﷺ is the second source of Islamic law. Whatever the Holy Prophet ﷺ said or did in his capacity of a Messenger is binding on the *Ummah*. This authority of the *Sunnah* is based on the revelation he received form Allah. Hence, the obedience of the Holy Prophet ﷺ is another from of the obedience of Allah. This prophetic authority which is established through a large number of Quranic verses, cannot be curtailed, neither by limiting its tenure, nor by exempting the worldly affairs from its scope.

CHAPTER 3

The Authenticity of the "Sunnah": its historical aspect

Faced with the overwhelming arguments in favour of the authority of Sunnah some people resort to another way of suspecting its credibility, that is, to suspect its historical authenticity.

According to them, the Sunnah of the Holy Prophet though having a binding authority for all times to come, has not been preserved in a trustworthy manner. Unlike the Holy Quran, they say, there is no single book containing reliable reports about the Sunnah. There are too many works having a large number of traditions sometimes conflicting each other. And those books, too, were compiled in the third century of Hijrah. So, we cannot place our trust in the reports which have not even been reduced to writing during the first three centuries.

This argument is based on a number of misstatements and misconceptions. As we shall see in this chapter, inshallah, it is totally wrong to claim that the traditions of the Sunnah have been complied in the third century. But, before approaching this historical aspect of the Sunnah, let us examine the argument in it's logical perspective.

This argument accepts that the Holy Prophet ﷺ has a prophetic authority for all times to come, and that his obedience is mandatory for all Muslims of whatever age, but in the same breath it claims that the reports of the Sunnah being unreliable, we cannot carry out this obedience. Does it not logically conclude that Allah has enjoined upon us to obey the Messenger, but did not make this obedience practicable. The question is whether Allah Almighty may give us a positive command to do something which is beyond our ability and means. The answer is certainly "no". The Holy Quran itself says,

لاَ يُكَلِّفُ اللهُ نَفساً إلاَّ وُسعَهَا

Allah does not task anybody except to his ability.

It cannot be envisaged that Allah will bind all the people with something which does not exist or cannot be ascertained. Accepted that, Allah has enjoined upon us to follow the Sunnah of the Holy Prophet, it certainly implies that the Sunnah is not undiscoverable. If Allah has made it obligatory to follow the Sunnah, He has certainly preserved it for us, in a reliable form.

The following aspect also merits consideration. Allah Almighty has given us a promise in the Holy Quran.

إِنَّا نَحنُ نَزَّلْنَا الذِّكْرَ وَإِنَّا لَهُ لَحَافِظُونَ (الحجر:٩)

Indeed we have revealed the *Zikr*, (i.e the Quran) and surely we will preserve it (15:9)

In this verse, Almighty Allah, has assured the preservation of the Holy Quran. This implies that the Quran will remain uninterpolated and that it shall always be transferred from one generation to the other in it's real and original form, undistorted by any foreign element. The question now is whether this divine protection is restricted only to the words of the Holy Quran or does it extend to its real meanings as well. If the prophetic explanation is necessary to understand the Holy Quran correctly, as proved in the first chapter then the preservation of the Quranic words alone cannot serve the purpose unless the prophetic explanations are also preserved. As quoted earlier, the Holy Book says,

إِنَّا أَنزلناإليك الذِّكْرَ لِتُبَيِّنَ لِلنَّاسِ مَا نُزِّلَ إِلَيهِم

We have revealed to you the Zikr (the Quran) so that you may explain to the people what has been sent down for them.

The word 'Zikr' has been used here for the Holy Quran as has been used in the verse 15:9 and it has been made clear that the "people" can only benefit from its guidance when they are led by the explantions of the Holy Prophet ﷺ.

Again the words "for the people" indicate (especially in the original Arabic context), that the Holy Prophet's explanation is always needed by "everyone".

Now, if everyone, in every age is in need of the prophetic explanation, without which they cannot fully benefit from the Holy Book, how would it be useful for them to preserve the Quranic text and leave it's prophetic explanation at the mercy of distorters, extending to it no type of protection whatsoever.

Therefore, once the necessity of the prophetic explanations of the Holy Quran is accepted, it will be self-contradictory to claim that these explanations are unavailable today. It will amount to negating the divine wisdom, because it is in no way a wise policy to establish the necessity of the Sunnah on the one hand, and to make its discovery impossible on the other. Such a policy cannot be attributed to Allah, the All-Mighty, the All-Wise.

This deductive argument is, in my view, sufficient to establish that comprehending the "Sunnah" of the Holy Prophet, which is necessay for the correct understanding of the divine guidance, shall as a whole, remain available in a reliable manner forever. All objections raised against the authenticity of the Sunnah as a whole, can be repudiated on this score alone. But in order to study the actual facts, we are giving here a brief account of the measures taken by the ummah to preserve the Sunnah of the Holy Prophet. It is a brief and an inductive study of the subject, for which the comprehensive and voluminous books are available in Arabic and other languages. The brief account we intend to give here is not comprehensive. The only purpose is to highlight some basic facts which if studied objectively, are well enough to support the deductive inference about the authenticity of the Sunnah.

The Preservation of Sunnah

It is totally wrong to say that the Sunnah of the Holy Prophet ﷺ was compiled for the first time in the third century. In fact, the compilation had begun in the very days of the Holy Prophet ﷺ as we shall see later, though the compilations in a written form were not the sole measures adopted for the preservation of the Sunnah. There were many other reliable sources of preservation also. In order to understand the point correctly we will have to know the different kinds of the Sunnah of the Holy Prophet ﷺ .

Three kinds of Ahadith

An individual tradition which narrates a 'Sunnah' of the Holy Prophet ﷺ is termed in the relevant sciences as 'Hadith' (Pl. Ahadith) The 'Ahadith', with regard to the frequency of their sources, are divided into three major kinds:

1- *Mutawatir*: It is a hadith narrated in each era, from the days of the Holy Prophet upto this day by such a large number of narrators that it is impossible to reasonably accept that all of them have colluded to tell a lie.

This kind is further classified into two sub-divisions:

(a) *Mutawatir in words*: It is a hadith whose words are narrated by such a large number as is required for a mutawatir, in a manner that all the narrators are unanimous in reporting it with the same words without any substantial discrepancy.

(b) *Mutawatir in meaning:* It is a mutawatir hadith which is not reported by the narrators in the same words. The words of the narrators are different. Sometimes even the reported events are not the same. But all the narrators are unanimous in reporting a basic concept which is common in all the reports. This common concept is also ranked as a *mutawatir* concept.

For example, there is a saying of the Holy Prophet ﷺ

مَنْ كَذَبَ عَلَيَّ مُتَعَمِّداً فَلْيَتَبَوَّأْ مقعده مِنَ النَّارِ

Whoever intentionally attributes a lie against me, should prepare his seat in the Fire.

This is a mutawatir hadith of the first kind, because it has a minimum of seventy four narrators. In other words, seventy four companions of the Holy Prophet ﷺ have reported this hadith at different occasions, all with the same words.

The number of those who received this hadith from these companions is many times greater, because each of the seventy four companions has conveyed it to a number of his pupils. Thus, the total number of the narrators of this hadith has been increasing in each successive generation, and has never been less than seventy four. All these narrators, who are now hundreds in number, report it in the same words without even a minor change. This hadith is, therefore, *mutawatir* by words, because it cannot be imagined reasonably that such a large number of people have colluded to coin a fallacious sentence in order to attribute it to the Holy Prophet ﷺ.

On the other hand, it is also reported by such a large number of narrators that the Holy Prophet ﷺ has enjoined us to perform two *Rak'at* in Fajr, four Rak'at in Zuhr, 'Asr and 'Isha, and three Rak'at in the Maghrib Prayer, yet the narrations of all the reporters who reported the number of Rak'at are not in the same words. Their words are different. Even the events reported by them are different. But the common feature of all the reports is the same. This common feature, namely, the exact number of Rak'at, is said to be mutawatir in meaning.

2. The second kind of hadith is *Mashhoor*. This term is defined by the scholars of Hadith as follows:

> "A hadith which is not *mutawatir*, but its narrators are not less than three in any generation" (1).

The same term is also used by the scholars of Fiqh, but their definition is slightly different. They say,

"A *mashhoor* hadith is one which was not mutawatir in the generation of the Holy Companions, but became mutawatir immediately after them (2).

The *Mashhoor* hadith according to each definition falls in the second category following the mutawatir.

3. *Khabarul wahid.* It is a hadith whose narrators are less than three in any given generation.

Let us now examine each kind separately:

The authenticity of the first two kinds

As for the *mutawatir*, nobody can question its authenticity. The fact narrated by a *mutawatir* chain is always accepted as an absolute truth even if pertaining to our daily life. Any statement based on a *mutawatir* narration must be accepted by everyone without any hesitation. I have never seen the city of Moscow, but the fact that Moscow is a large city and is the capital of U S S R is an absolute truth which cannot be denied. This fact is proved, to

(1) Tadreeburrawi, by Suyuti P. 181 V.2, Karachi 1972.

(2) أصول السرخسي

me, by a large number of narrators who have seen the city. This is a continuously narrated or a *mutawatir* fact which cannot be denied or questioned.

I have not seen the events of the First and the Second World War. But the fact that these two wars occured, stands proved, without a shadow of doubt on the basis of the mutawatir reports about them. Nobody with a sound sense can claim that all those who reported the occurance of these two wars have colluded to coin a fallacious report and that no war took place at all. This strong belief in the factum of war is based on the *mutawatir* reports of the event.

In the same way the mutawatir reports about the Sunnah of the Holy Prophet ﷺ are to be held as absolutely true without any iota of doubt in their authenticity. The authenticity of the Holy Quran being the same Book as that revealed to the Holy Prophet ﷺ is of the same nature. Thus, the *mutawatir ahadith*, whether they be mutawatir in words or in meaning, are as authentic as the Holy Quran, and there is no difference between the two in as far as the reliability of their source of narration is concerned.

Although the *ahadith* falling under the first category of the mutawatir, i.e. the *mutawatir* in words, are very few in number, yet the a*hadith* relating to the second kind, namely, the *mutawatir* in meaning, are available in large numbers. Thus, a very sizeable portion of the Sunnah of the Holy Prophet ﷺ falls in this kind of mutawatir, the authenticity of which cannot be doubted in any manner.

As for the second kind, i.e. the *Mashhoor* , its standard of authenticity is lower than that of the *mutawatir*; yet, it is sufficient to provide satisfaction about the correctness of the narration because it's narrators have been more than three trustworthy persons in every generation.

The third kind is *Khabarul wahid*. The authenticity of this kind depends on the veracity of its narrators. If the narrator is trustworthy in all respects, the report given by him can be accepted, but if the single reporter is believed to be doubtful, the entire report subsequently remains doubtful. This principle is followed in every sphere of life. Why should it not be applied to the reports about the Sunnah of the Holy Prophet ﷺ ? Rather, in the case of 'Ahadith', this principle is most applicable, because the reporters of ahadith were fully cognizant of the delicate nature of what they narrate. It was not simple news of an ordinary event having no legal or religious effect. It was the narration of a fact which has a far-reaching effect on the lives of millions of people. The reporters of Ahadith knew well that it is not a play to ascribe a word or act to the Holy Prophet ﷺ. Any deliberate error in this narration, or any negligence in this respect would lead them to the wrath of Allah and render them liable to be punished in hell. Every reporter of *hadith* was aware of the following well-known mutawatir hadith:

مَنْ كَذَبَ عَلَيَّ مُتَعَمِّداً فَلْيَتَبَوَّأْ مَقْعَدَهُ مِنَ النَّارِ

Whoever attributes a lie to me, he should prepare his seat in the Fire.

This hadith had created such a strong sense of responsibility in the hearts of the narrators of ahadith that while reporting anything about the Holy Prophet ﷺ they often turned pale out of fear, lest some error should creep into their narration.

This was the basic reason for which the responsible narrators of *ahadith* showed the maximum precaution in preserving and reporting a *hadith*. This standard of precaution cannot be found in any other reports of historical events. So, the principle that the veracity of a report depends on the nature of its reporter is far more validly applicable to the reports of *ahadith* than it is applicable to the general reports of ordinary nature.

Let us now examine the various ways adopted by the *Ummah* to preserve the *ahadith* in their original form:

Different ways of Ahadith Preservation

As we shall later see, the companions of the Holy Prophet ﷺ reduced a large number of ahadith in writing. Yet, writing was not the sole means of their preservation. There were many other ways.

1- Memorization

First of all the companions of the Holy Prophet ﷺ used to learn *ahadith* by heart. The Holy Prophet ﷺ has said:

نضّر الله عبدا سمع مقالتی فوعاها ثمّ أدّاها کما سمع

> May Allah bestow vigor to a person who hears my saying and learns it by heart, then conveys it to others exactly as he hears it.

The companions of the Holy Prophet ﷺ were eager to follow this *hadith* and used to devout considerable time for commiting *ahadith* to their memories. A large number of them left their homes and began to live in the Mosque of the Holy Prophet ﷺ so that they may hear the *ahadith* directly from the mouth of the Holy Prophet. They spent all their time exclusively in securing the ahadith in their hearts. They are called *Ashab al-suffah.*

The Arabs had such strong memories that they would easily memorize hundreds of verses of their poetry. Nearly all of them knew by heart detailed pedigrees of not only themselves, but also of their horses and camels. Even their children had enough knowledge of the pedigrees of different tribes. Hammad is a famous narrator of the Arab Poetry. It is reported that he knew by heart one hundred long poems for each letter from the alphabet, meaning thereby that he knew three thousand and thirty eight long poems (1).

The Arabs were so proud of their memory power that they placed more of their confidence on it than on writing. Some poets deemed it a blemish to preserve their poetry in writing. They believed that writings on papers can be tampered with, while the memory cannot be distorted by any one. If any poets have written some of their poems, they did not like to disclose this fact, because it would be indicative of a defect in their memory (2).

The companions of the Holy Prophet ﷺ utilised this memory for preserving *ahadith* which they deemed to be the only source of guidance after the Holy Quran. It is obvious that their enthusiasm towards the preservation of *ahadith* far exceeded their zeal for preserving their poetry and literature. They therefore, used their memory in respect of *ahadith* with more vigor and more precaution.

Sayyiduna *Abu Hurairah,* the famous companion of the Holy Prophet ﷺ, who has reported 5374 ahadith, says,

جزأتُ الليل ثلاثة أجزاء، ثلثا أصلى، وثلثا أنام، وثلثا أذكر فيه حديث رسول الله ﷺ

> I have divided my night into three parts. In one third of the night I perform salaah, in one third I sleep and in one third I memorize the ahadith of the Holy Prophet ﷺ (3).

Sayyiduna *Abu Hurairah*, after embracing Islam, devoted his life exclusively for learning the *ahadith*. He has reported more *ahadith* than any other companion of the Holy Prophet ﷺ.

---

(1) Al-a'lam by zrikli 2:131

(2) See Al-aghani V. 61 P. 611

(3) سنن الدارمي ج ١ ص ٨٢ والجامع لأخلاق الراوي للخطيب ص ١٨٠ .

Once Marwan, the governor of Madinah, tried to test his memory. He invited him to his house where he asked him to narrate some *ahadith*. Marwan simultaneously ordered his scribe *Abu Zu'aizi'ah* to sit behind a curtain and write the *ahadith* reported by *Abu Hurairah* رضى الله عنه. The scribe noted the *ahadith*. After a year he invited *Abu Hurairah* again and requested him to repeat what he narrated last year, and likewise ordered *Abu Zu'aizi'ah* to sit behind a curtain and compare the present words of *Abu Hurairah* with the *ahadith* he had already written previously. *Sayyiduna Abu Hurairah* began to repeat the *ahadith* while *Abu Zu'aizi'ah* compared them. He found that *Abu Hurairah* did not leave a single word, nor did he change any word from his earlier narrations (1).

Numerous other examples of this type are available in the history of the science of *hadith* which clearly show that the *ahadith* reporters have used their extra-ordinary memory power given to them by Allah Almighty for preserving the Sunnah of the Holy Prophet ﷺ, as promised by Him in the Holy Quran.

As we shall later see, scholars of the science of *hadith* developed the science of *Asma'ur-rijal* by which they have deduced reliable means to test the memory power of each narrator of *ahadith*. They never accepted any *hadith* as reliable unless all of it's narrators were proved to have high memory standards.

Thus, "memory-power" in the science of *hadith* is not a vague term of general nature. It is a technical term having specified criteria to test the veracity of narrators. A great number of scholars of the sciences of "*Asma'urrijal*" and "*Jarh and Ta'dil*" have devoted their lives to examine the reporters of hadith on that criteria. Their task was to judge the memory power of each narrator and to record objective opinions about them.

Memories of the *ahadith* reporters cannot be compared with

---

(1). البداية والنهاية ص ١٠٦ ج ٨ وسير أعلام النبلاء للذهبي ص ٤٣١ ج ٢

the memory of a layman today who witnesses an event or hears some news and conveys it to others in a careless manner seldom paying due attention to the correctness of his narration. The follows points in this respect are worth mentioning:

1. The reporters of *ahadith* were fully cognizant of the great importance and the delicate nature of what they intended to report. They whole-heartedly believed that any misstatement or negligent reporting in this field would cause them to be condemned both in this world and in the Hereafter. This belief equipped them with a very strong sense of responsibility. It is evident that such a strong sense of responsibility makes a reporter more accurate in his reports. A newsman reporting an accident of a common nature in which common people are involved, can report it's details with less accuracy. But if the accident involves the President or the Prime Minister of his country, he will certainly show more diligence, precaution and shall employ his best ability to report the incident as accurately as possible. The reporter is the same, but in the second case he is more accurate in his report than he was in the first case, because the nature of the incident has made him more responsible, hence more cautious.

It cannot be denied that the companions of the Holy Prophet ﷺ, their pupils and other reliable narrators of *ahadith* believed with their heart and soul that the importance of a hadith attributed to the Holy Prophet ﷺ exceeds the importance of any other report whatsoever. They believed that it is a source of Islamic law which will govern the Ummah for all times to come. They believed that any negligence in this respect will lead them to the severe punishment of hell. So, their sense of responsibility while reporting *ahadith* was far higher than that of a newsman reporting an important incident about the head of his country.

2. The interest of the reporter in the reported events and his ability to understand them correctly is another important factor which affects the accuracy of his report. If the reporter is indifferent or negligent about what he reports, little reliability can

be placed on his memory or on any subsequent report based on it. But if the reporter is not only honest, serious and intelligent but also interested and involved in the event, his report can easily be relied upon.

If some proceedings are going on in a court of law,the reports of these proceedings can be of different kinds. One report was given by a layman from the audience who was incidentally present at the court. He had neither any interest in the proceedings nor had due knowledge and understanding of the legal issues involved. He gathered a sketchy picture of the proceedings and reported it to a third person. Such a report can neither be relied upon nor taken as an authentic version of the proceedings. This report may be full of errors because the reporter lacks the ability to understand the matter correctly and the responsible attitude to report it accurately. Such a reporter may not only err in his reporting, but may after some time also forget the proceedings altogether.

Suppose, there are some newsmen also who have witnessed the proceedings for the purpose of reporting them in their newspapers. They have more knowledge and understanding than a layman of the first kind. Their report shall be more correct than that of the former. But despite their interest and intelligence, they are not fully aware of the technical and legal questions involved in the proceedings. Their report shall thus, remain deficient in the legal aspect of the proceedings and cannot be relied upon to the that extent because despite their good memory, they cannot grasp the legal issues completely.

There were also lawyers who were directly involved in the proceedings. They participated in the debate at the bar. They have argued the case. They were fully aware of the delicate legal issues involved. They understood each and every sentence expressed by other lawyers and the judge. It is obvious that the report of the proceedings given by these lawyers shall be the most authentic one. Having full knowledge and understanding of the case they can neither forget nor err while reporting the substantial and material parts of the proceedings.

Suppose, all the three categories had the same standard of memory power. Yet, the facts narrated by them have different levels of correctness. It shows that the interest of the reporter in the reported event and his understanding of the facts involved plays an important role in making his memory more effective and accurate.

The deep interest of the companions of the Holy Prophet ﷺ in his sayings and acts, rather even in his gesture is beyond any doubt. Their understanding of what he said, and their close knowledge and observation of the background and environment under which he spoke or acted cannot be questioned. Thus, all the basic factors which help mobilize one's memory were present in them.

3. The standard of memory power required for the authenticity of a report is not, as mentioned earlier, a vague concept for which no specific criteria exist. The scholars of the Science of *hadith* have laid down hard and fast rules to ascertain the memory standard of each reporter. Unless a reporter of a *hadith* has specific standards of memory, his reports are not accepted as reliable.

4. There is a big difference between memorizing a fact which incidentally came to the knowledge of someone who never cared to remember it any more, and memorizing of a fact which is learnt by someone with eagerness, with an objective purpose to remember it and with a constant effort to keep it in memory.

While I studied Arabic, my teacher told me many things which I do not remember today. But the vocabulary I learnt from my teacher is secured in my mind. The reason is obvious. I never cared to keep the former remembered, while I was very much eager to learn the latter by heart and to store it in my memory.

The companions of the holy Prophet ﷺ did not listen to him incidentally nor were they careless in remembering what they heard. Instead, they daily spared specific times for learning the *ahadith* by heart. The example of *Abu Hurairah* رضی الله عنه has already been cited. He used to spare one third of every night in repeating the *ahadith* he learnt from the Holy Prophet ﷺ.

Thus, memorization was not a weaker source of preservation of *ahadith*, as sometimes is presumed by those who have no proper knowledge of the science of hadith. Looked at in its true perspective, the memories of the reliable reporters of *ahadith* were no less reliable a source of preservation than compiling the ahadith in book form.

2. Discussions

The second source of preservation of ahadith was by mutual discussions held by the companions of the Holy Prophet ﷺ. Whenever they came to know of a new sunnah, they used to narrate it to others. Thus all the companions would tell each other what they learnt from the Holy Prophet ﷺ. This was to comply with the specific directions given by the Holy Prophet ﷺ in this respect. Here are some *ahadith* to this effect:

ليبلّغ الشّاهد الغائبَ

Those present should convey (my sunnah) to those absent (1).

بلّغوا عنّى ولو آية

Convey to others on my behalf, even though it be a single verse (2).

---

(1). صحيح البخاري كتاب المناسك باب الخطبة أيام منى

(2). صحيح البخاري كتاب الأنبياء ، باب ما ذكر عن بني إسرائيل

نضّر الله امرأ سمعَ منّا حديثا فحفظَه حتّى يبلغه غيره

May Allah grant vigor to a person who listens to my saying and learns it by heart until he conveys it to others (1).

تسمعون ويُسمَع منكم، ويسمع ممّن يسمع منكم

You hear (my sayings) and others will hear from you, then others will hear from them (2).

ما أفادَ المسلم أخاه فائدة أحسن من حديث حسن بلغه فبلّغه

A Muslim cannot offer his brother a better benefit than transmitting to him a good *hadith* which has reached him (3).

These directions given by the Holy Prophet ﷺ were more than sufficient to induce his companions towards acquiring the knowledge of *ahadith* and to convey them to others.

The Holy Prophet ﷺ also motivated his companions to study the *ahadith* in their meetings. The word used for this study is*Tadarus* which means "to teach each other". One person would narrate a particular *hadith* to the other, in turn, would repeat it to the first, and so on. The purpose was to learn it correctly. Each one would listen to the other's version and correct his mistake, if any.The result of this *ttadarus* (discussion) was to remember the *ahadith* as firmly as possible. The Holy Prophet ﷺ has held this described process of tadarus to be more meritorious with Allah than the individual worship throughout in the night. He has said.

---

(1). جامع الترمذي كتاب العلم حديث ٢٦٥٨ وسنن أبي داود حديث ٣٦٦٠

(2). سنن أبي داود كتاب العلم باب فضل نشر العلم حديث ٣٦٥٩

(3). جامع بيان العلم لابن عبد البر ص٤٣ ج ١

تدارُسُ العلم ساعة من الليل خير من إحيائها

> *Tadarus* of knowledge (1) for any period of time in the night, is better than spending the entire night in worship (2).

Moreover, the Holy Prophet ﷺ has also warned, that it is a major sin to hide a word of 'knowledge' whenever it is asked for:

من سُئِلَ علما يعلمُه فكتمه ألجم بلجام من نار

> Whoever is questioned pertaining to such knowledge that he has and thereafter conceals it, will be bridled by a rein of fire (3).

At another occasion the Holy Prophet ﷺ disclosed that concealment of 'knowledge' is in itself a major sin, even though the person having that knowledge is not asked about it. He said:

من كتمَ علما ينتفع به جاء يوم القيامة ملجما بلجام من نار

> Whoever conceals knowledge which can be benefitted from, will come on Doomsday bridled with a bridle of fire (4).

The *hadith* makes it clear that the disclosure of knowledge is an inherent obligation on each knowledgeable person, no matter whether he is asked about it or not.

As the knowledge of the sunnah of the Holy Prophet ﷺ was the highest branch of knowledge in the eyes of his companions, they deemed it an indispensible obligation on their shoulders to convey to others what they knew of the sunnah.

Thus, it was the most favourite hobby of the companions of

---

(1) The word " Knowledge" in the era of Nabi ﷺ was used to connote knowledge relative to the Holy Qur'an and the hadith.

(2). جامع بيان العلم لابن عبد البر

(3). جامع الترمذي كتاب العلم حديث ٢٦٥١

(4). جامع بيان العلم لابن عبد البر

the Holy Prophet ﷺ whenever they sat together, instead of being involved in useless talks, to discuss his sayings and acts. Each of them would mention what he knew while the others would listen and try to learn it by heart.

These frequent discussions have played an important role in the preservation of the Sunnah. It was by the virtue of these discussions that the *ahadith* known only by some individuals were conveyed to others, and the circle of narrators was gradually enlarged. Since these discussions were carried out at a time when the Holy Prophet ﷺ was himself present among them, they had the full opportunity to confirm the veracity of what has been conveyed to them in this process, and some of them actually did so. The result was that the knowledge of *ahadith* acquired a wide range among the companions, which not only helped in spreading the knowledge of Sunnah but also provided a check on the mistakes of narrations, because if someone forgets some part of a *hadith*, the others were present to fill in the gap and to correct the error.

3. Practice

The third way of preservation of the Sunnah was to bring it into practice.

The knowledge of Sunnah was not merely a theoretical knowledge, nor were the teachings of the Holy Prophet ﷺ merely philosophical. They related to practical life. The Holy Prophet ﷺ did not confine himself to giving lessons and sermons only, he also trained his companions practically. Whatever they learnt from the Holy Prophet ﷺ they spared no effort to bring it into actual practice. Each companion was so enthusiastic in practicing the Sunnah of the Holy Prophet ﷺ, that he tried his best to imitate even his personal habits.

Thus the whole atmosphere was one of following the

Sunnah. The Sunnah was not a verbal report only, it was a living practice, a widespred behavior and a current fashion demonstrating itself everywhere in the society, in all the affairs of their daily life.

If a student of mathematics confines himself with remembering the formulas orally, he is likely to forget them after a lapse of time, but if he brings them in practice, ten times a day, he shall never forget them.

Likewise, the Sunnah was not an oral service carried out by the companions . They brought it into their daily practice. The Sunnah was the centre of gravity for all their activities. How could they forget the Sunnah of the Holy Prophet ﷺ around which they built the structure of their whole lives?

Thus, constant practice in accordance with the dictates of the Sunnah was another major factor which advanced the process of preserving the Sunnah and protected it from the foreign elements aiming at its distortion.

4. Writing

The fourth way of preserving of *ahadith* was writing. Quite a large number of the companions of the Holy Prophet ﷺ reduced the *ahadith* in writing after hearing them from the Holy Prophet ﷺ.

It is true that in the beginning the Holy Prophet ﷺ had forbidden some of his companions from writing anything other then the verses of the Holy Quran. However, this prohibition was not because the *ahadith* had no authoritative value, but because the Holy Prophet ﷺ had in the same breath ordered them to narrate his *ahadith* orally. The full text of the relevant hadith is as follows:

لا تكتبوا عنّى، ومن كتبَ عنّى غير القرآن فليمحه، حدّثوا عنّى ولا حرج، ومن كذب علىّ متعمّدا فليتبوّأ مقعده من النّار

Do not write (what you hear) from me, and whoever has written something (he heard) from me, he should rub it. Narrate to others (what you hear) from me; and whoever deliberately attributes a lie to me , he should prepare his seat in the Fire" (1).

The underlined phrase of the hadith clarifies that prohibition for writing *hadith* was not on account of negating it's authority. The actual reason was that in the beginning of the revelation of the Holy Quran, the companions of the Holy Prophet ﷺ were not fully familiar with the Quranic style, nor was the Holy Quran compiled in a separate book form. In those days some companions began to write the *ahadith* alongwith the Quranic text. Some explanations of the Holy Quran given by the Holy Prophet ﷺ were written by some of them mixed with the Quranic verses without any distinction between the two. It was therefore feared that it would lead to confuse the Quranic text with the *ahadith*.

It was in this background that the Holy Prophet ﷺ stopped this practice and ordered that anything written other than the Holy Quran should be rubbed or omitted. It should be kept in mind that in those days there was a great shortage of writing paper. Even the verses of the Holy Quran used to be written on pieces of leather, on planks of wood, on animal bones and sometimes on stones. It was much difficult to compile all those thengs in a book form, and if the ahadith were also written in the like manner it would be more difficult to distinguish between the

---

(1) See Sahih of Muslim V.2.P 414.

writings of the Holy Quran and those of the ahadith. The lack of familiarity with the Quranic style would also help creating confusion.

For these reasons the Holy Prophet ﷺ directed his companions to abstain from writing the *ahadith* and to confine their preservation to the first three ways which were equally reliable as discussed earlier.

But all this was in the earlier period of his prophethood. When the companions became fully conversant of the style of the Holy Quran and writing paper became available, this transitory measure of precaution was taken back, because the danger of confusion between the Quran and the *hadith* no longer existed.

At this stage, the Holy Prophet ﷺ himself directed his companions to write down the *ahadith*. Some of his instructions in this respect are quoted below:

1. One companion from the *Ansar* complained to the Holy Prophet ﷺ that he hears from him some *ahadith*, but he sometimes forgets them. The Holy Prophet ﷺ said:

استعِن بيمينك وأومأ بيده لخط

"Seek help from your right hand and pointed out to a writing (1).

2. *Rafe' ibn Khadij* رضي الله عنه the famous companion of the Holy Prophet says. "I said to the Holy Prophet ﷺ we hear from you many things, should we write them down?" He replied:

اكتبوا، ولا حرج

You may wirte.There is no harm (2).

---

(1).جامع الترمذي ص١٠٧ ج ٢

(2). تدريب الراوي ص ٢٨٦ والمحدث الفاصل ص ٣٦٩

(3) Sayyiduna Anas رضي الله عنه reports that the Holy Prophet ﷺ has said:

قيّدوا العلم بالكتاب

"Preserve knowledge by writing (1).

4. Sayyiduna *Abu Rafe'* sought permission from the Holy Prophet ﷺ to write *ahadith*. The Holy Prophet ﷺ permitted him to do so (2).

It is reported that the *ahadith* written by *Abu Rafe* رضي الله عنه were copied by other companions, too. *Salma*, a pupil of Ibn Abbas says:

رأيتُ عبد الله بن عبّاس معه ألواح يكتُب عليها عن أبى رافع شيئا من فعل رسول الله ﷺ

I saw some small wooden boards with Abdullah Ibn Abbas. He was writing on them some reports of the acts of the Holy Prophet ﷺ which he acquired from *Abu Rafe* (3).

5. Abdullah ibn 'Amr ibn al-'Aas reports that the Holy Prophet ﷺ said to him:

قيّدوا العلم

Preserve knowledge.

He asked "and how should it be preserved?". The Holy Prophet ﷺ replied "writing it" (4).

In other report he says,

---

(1). جامع بيان العلم لابن عبد البر ص ٧٢ ج١ والمحدث الفاصل ص ٣٦٨

(2). جامع الترمذي ص ١٠٧ ج٢

(3). طبقات ابن سعد ص ٣٧١ ج٢

(4). قلت : وما تقييده؟ قال: كتابته (مستدرك الحاكم ص ١٠٦ ج ١ وجامع بيان العلم ص٧٣ ج١

"I came to the Holy Prophet ﷺ and told him" I want to narrate your *ahadith*. So, I want to take assistance of my handwriting beside my heart. Do you deem it fit for me? "The Holy Prophet ﷺ replied, "If it is my *hadith* you may seek help from your hand besides your heart" (1).

6. It was for this reason that he used to write *ahadith* frequently. He himself says,

كنت أكتب كلّ شئ أسمعه من رسول الله ﷺ وأريد حفظه، فنهتني قريش، وقالوا: أتكتب كلّ شئ تسمعه من رسول الله ﷺ وإنما هو بشر يغضَب كما يغضَب البشر.

I used to write whatever I heard from the Holy Prophet ﷺ and wanted to learn it by heart. Some people of the Quresh dissuaded me and said, "Do you write every thing you hear from the Holy Prophet ﷺ, while he is a human being and sometimes he may be in anger as any other human beings may be?" (2).

They meant that the Holy Prophet ﷺ might say something in a state of anger which he did not seriously intend. So, one should be selective in writing his ahadith. 'Abdullah ibn Amr conveyed their opinion to the Holy Prophet ﷺ. In reply the Holy Prophet ﷺ pointed to his lips and said,

والذي نفس محمد بيده ما يخرج مما بينهما إلا حق، فاكتب

I swear by the One in whose hands is the soul of

---

(1). سنن الدارمي ، باب ٤٣ ص ١٠٤ ج ١

(2). سنن أبي داود ، كتاب العلم ص ١٥٦ ، ١٥٧ ج٢

Muhammad , nothing comes out from these two (lips) except truth. So, do write.(1)

It was a clear and absolute order given by the Holy Prophet to write each and every saying of him without any hesitation or doubt about it's authoritative nature.

In compliance to this order, 'Abdullah ibn 'Amr wrote a large number of *ahadith* and compiled them in a book form which he named "*Al Sahifah al Sadiqah*". Some details about this book shall be discussed later on inshaallah.

7. During the conquest of *Makkah* (8 A.H.) the Holy Prophet ﷺ delivered a detailed sermon containing a number of Shariah imperatives, including human rights. One Yemenite person from the gathering, namely, Abu Shah requested the Holy Prophet ﷺ to provide him the sermon in a written form. The Holy Prophet ﷺ thereafter ordered his companions as follows:-

اكتبوا لأبى شاه

Write it down for Abu Shah (2).

These seven examples are more than sufficient to prove that writing of ahadith was not only permitted but also ordered by the Holy Prophet ﷺ and that the earlier bar against writing was only for a transitory period to avoid any possible confusion between the verses of the Holy Quran and the *ahadith*. After this transitory period the fear of confusion ended, the bar was lifted and the companions were persuaded to preserve ahadith in a written form.

---

(1) سنن أبي داود ج ٢ ص ٥١٣ وطبقات ابن سعد ج ٤ ص ٢٦٢ ومستدرك الحاكم ج١ ص ١٠٥ و١٠٦ والمحدث الفاصل ص ٣٦٤ - ٣٦٦ .

(2) صحيح البخاري كتاب العلم ، باب كتابة العلم ص ٢٢ ج١ .

THE COMPILATION OF HADITH IN THE DAYS OF THE HOLY PROPHET ﷺ

We have discussed the different methods undertaken by the companions of the Holy Prophet ﷺ to preserve the *ahadith*. An objective study of these methods would prove that although 'writing' was not the sole method of their preservation, yet it was never neglected in this process. Inspired by the Holy Prophet ﷺ himself, a large number of his companions used to secure the *ahadith* in written form.

When we study individual efforts of the companions for compiling *ahadith*, we find that thousands of *ahadith* were written in the very days of the Holy Prophet ﷺ and his Four Caliphs. It is not possible to give an exhaustive survey of these efforts, for it will require a separate voluminous book on the subject which is not intended here. Nevertheless, we propose to give a brief account of some outstanding compilations of *ahadith* in that early period. It will, at least, refute the misconception that the *ahadith* were not complied during the first three centuries.

THE DICTATIONS OF THE HOLY PROPHET ﷺ

To begin with, we would refer to the fact that a considerable number of *ahadith* were dictated and directed to be secured in written form by the Holy Prophet himself. Here are some examples:

THE BOOK OF SADAQAH

1. The Holy Prophet ﷺ has dictated detailed documents containing rules of shari'ah about the levy of *zakah*, and specifying the quantum and the rate of *Zakah* in respect of different zakatable assets. This document was named "*Kitab al Sadaqah*" (The Book of Sadaqah). Abdullah ibn 'Umar says:

كتبَ رسول الله ﷺ كتاب الصدقة فلم يخرجه إلى عمّاله حتّى قبض، فقرنه بسيفه فلمّا قبض عمل به أبو بكر حتى قبض، وعمِلَ به حتى قبض، وكان فيه: فى خمس من الإبل شاة

The Holy Prophet ﷺ dictated the Book of Sadaqah and was yet to send it to his governors when he passed away. He had attached it to his sword. When he passed away, *Abu-Bakr* acted according to it till he passed away, then *Umar* acted according to it till he passed away. It was mentioned in his book that one goat is leviable on five camels.............." (1).

The text of this document is available in several books of *ahadith* like the *Sunan* of *Abu Dawood*. Imam Zuhri, the renowned scholar of hadith used to teach this document to his pupils. He used to say:

"This is the text of the document dictated by the Holy Prophet ﷺ about the rules of *Sadaqah* (Zakah). Its original manuscript is with the children of Sayyiduna Umar. Salim, the grandson of Umar had taught it to me. I had learnt it by heart. Umar Ibn 'Abd-ul-'Aziz had procured a copy of this text from Salim and 'Abdullah, the grandsons of Umar. I have

---

(1) جامع الترمذي ، أبواب الزكوة، باب ما جاء فى زكوة الإبل ص ١٣٥.

the same copy with me (1).

The Script of Amr b. Hazm

In 10 A.H. when Najran was conquered by the Muslims, the Holy Prophet ﷺ appointed his companion *'Amr ibn Hazm* as governer of the province of Yemen. At this time the Holy Prophet ﷺ dictated a detailed book to *Ubayy ibn Ka'b* and handed it over to 'Amr ibn Hazm.

This book, besides some general advices, contained the rules of Shari'ah about purification, Salah, Zakah, Ushr, Hajj, Umrah, Jihad (battle), spoils, taxes, Diyah (blood money), administration, education etc.

Sayyiduna Amr ibn Hazm performed his functions as governor of Yemen in the light of this book. After his demise this document remained with his grandson, Abu Bakr, Imam Zuhri learnt and copied it from him. He used to teach it to his pupils(2).

WRITTEN DIRECTIVES TO OTHER GOVERNORS

Similarly, when the Holy Prophet ﷺ appointed some of his companions as governors of different provinces he used to dictate to them similar documents as his directives which they could follow in performing their duties as rulers or as judges. When he appointed Abu Huraira and *Ala'ibn al Hazrami* as his envoy to the Zoroastrians of Hajar, he dictated to them a directive containing certain rules of Shariah about *Zakah* and *Ushr* (3).

---

(1). سنن أبي داود ، كتاب الزكوة ص ٢١٨ - ٢٢٠ ج١

(2) Certain extracts of this book are found in the works of hadith. F^^or the full text see الوثائق السياسية في الإسلام للدكتور حميدالله ص ١٠٤ - ١٠٩ .

(3) . طبقات ابن سعد ج ١ ص ٢٦٣

Likewise, when he sent *Mu'az ibn Jabal* and *Malik ibn Murarah* to Yemen, he gave them a document dictated by him which contained certain rules of Shariah (1).

WRITTEN DIRECTIVES FOR CERTAIN DELEGATIONS

Certain Arab tribes who lived in remote areas far from Madinah, after embracing Islam used to send their delegations to the Holy Prophet ﷺ. These delegations used to stay at Madinah for a considerable period during which they would learn the teachings of Islam, read the Holy Quran and listen to the sayings of the Holy Prophet ﷺ. When they returned to their homes, some of them requested the Holy Prophet ﷺ to dictate some instructions for them and for their tribes. The Holy Prophet ﷺ used to accept this request and would dictate some directives containing such rules of Shari'ah as they most needed.

1. *Sayyiduna Wa'il ibn Hujr* came from Yemen and before leaving for home, requested the Holy Prophet ﷺ :

اكتُبْ لى إلى قومى كِتابا

Write me a book addressed to my tribe.

The Holy Prophet ﷺ dictated three documents to Sayyiduna Mu'awiyah. One of these documents pertained to personal problems of Wail ibn Hujr, while the other two consisted of certain general precepts of Shari'ah concerning *Salah*, *Zakah*, prohibition of liquorr, usury and certain other matters (2).

2. *Munqiz ibn Hayyan*, a member of the tribe of Abdulqais came to the Holy Prophet ﷺ and embraced Islam, while returning home he was given a written document by the Holy Prophet ﷺ which he carried to his tribe but initially he did not

---

(1). طبقات ابن سعد ج١ ص ٢٦٥

(2). طبقات ابن سعد ص ٢٨، ج ١ ، والوثائق السياسية رقم ١٣١ ص ١٢٦ - ١٣٠

disclose it to anyone. When, due to his efforts, his father-in-law embraced Islam, he handed over the document to him who in turn read it before his tribe which subsequently embraced Islam. It was after this, that the famous delegation of *Abdulqais* came to the Holy Prophet ﷺ . The detailed narration is found in the books of Bukhari and Muslim (1).

3. The delegation of the tribe of Ghamid came to the Holy Prophet ﷺ and embraced Islam. The Holy Prophet ﷺ sent them to Sayyiduna *Ubayy ibn Ka'b* who taught them the Holy Quran and:

وكتبَ لهم رسول الله ﷺ كتابا فيه شرائع الإسلام

the Holy Prophet ﷺ dictated for them a book containing injunctions of Islam (2).

4. The delegation of the tribe of Khath'am came to the Holy Prophet ﷺ . While discussing their arrival Ibn Sa'd reports on the authority of different reliable narrators.

فقالوا آمنا بالله ورسوله وما جاء من عند الله فاكتب
لنا كتابا نتّبع ما فيه، فكتب لهم كتابا شهد فيه جرير
بن عبد الله ومَن حضَرَ

They said, "We believe in Allah, His messenger and in whatever has come from Allah. So, write for us a document that we may follow." The Holy Prophet ﷺ wrote for them a document. *Jarir ibn Abdullah* and those present stood as witnesses to that document" (3).

5. The delegation of the tribes of *Sumalah* and Huddan

---

(1) المرقاة شرح المشكوة ص ٨٨ ج ١، وشرح النووي ص ٣٣ ج ١.

(2) طبقات ابن سعد ص ٣٤٥ ج ١ .

(3) طبقات ابن سعد ص ٣٤٨ ج ١ .

came after the conquest of Makkah. They embraced Islam. The Holy Prophet ﷺ dictated for them a document containing Islamic injunctions about *Zakah*. Sayyiduna *Sabit ibn Qais* had written the document and *Sa'd ibn Ubadah* and *Muhammad ibn Maslamah* stood as witnesses (1).

6. The same *Sabit ibn Qais* also wrote a document dictated by the Holy Prophet ﷺ for the delegation of the tribe of Aslam. The witnesses were *Abu Ubaidah ibn Jarrah and Umar ibn Khattab*.

These are only a few examples which are neither comprehensive nor exhaustive. Many other instances of the same nature are found in only one book, namely, the *Tabaqat* of *Ibn Sa'd*. A thorough research in all the relevant books would certainly expose a large number of like events for which a more detailed book is required.

All these examples refer to those events only where the Holy Prophet ﷺ dictated documents containing general Islamic injunctions. He has also dictated numerous official documents in individual cases. The large number of such documents prevents us from providing even a short reference to all of them in this brief study. All these documents also form part of the *Sunnah* and a large number of Islamic injunctions are inferred from them. In brevity, we instead would only refer to a work of Dr. Muhammad Hamidullah, namely, *Al-Wasaiq al Siyasiyyah*, in which he has compiled a considerable number of such documents. Those who desire further study may peruse the same.

---

(1). طبقات ابن سعد ص ۳۰۲ ج ۱

THE COMPILATIONS OF HADITH BY THE COMPANIONS OF THE HOLY PROPHET ﷺ

As discussed earlier, the Holy Prophet ﷺ has not only permitted but also pursuaded his companions to write down his ahadith. In pursuance of this direction, the blessed companions of the Holy Prophet ﷺ used to write *ahadith*, and a considerable number of them have compiled these writings in book forms. Some examples are given below:

THE SCRIPTS OF ABU HURAIRAH رضي الله عنه

It is well-known that *Abu Huraira* رضي الله عنه has narrated more *ahadith* than any other companion of the Holy Prophet ﷺ. The number of *ahadith* reported by him is said to be 5374. The reason was that he, after embracing Islam, devoted his full life for the sole purpose of bearing and preserving the *ahadith* of the Holy Prophet ﷺ. Unlike the other famous companions, he did not employ himself in any economic activity. He used to remain in the Mosque of the Holy Prophet ﷺ to hear what he said and to witness each event around him. He remained hungry, faced starvations and hardships. Yet, he did not leave the function he had undertaken.

There are concrete evidences that he had preserved the ahadith in written form. One of his pupils, namely, Hasan ibn 'Amr reports that once :

Abu Huraira رضي الله عنه took him to his home and showed him "many books" containing the ahadith of the Holy Prophet ﷺ (1).

It shows that Abu Hurairah had many scripts of ahadith

---

(1). جامع بيان العلم ص ١٧٤ ج ١ وفتح الباري ص ١٨٤ ج ١

with him. It is also established that a number of his pupils had prepared several scripts of his narrations.

The Script of Abdullah ibn Amr

It has been stated earlier that *Abdullah ibn 'Amr* was specifically instructed by Holy Prophet ﷺ to write ahadith. He therefore compiled a big script and named it "*Al sahifah al Sadiqah*" (The script of Truth). Abdullah ibn 'Amr was very precautious in preserving this script. Mujahid, one of his favorite pupils says, "I went to Abdullah ibn Amr and took in hand a script placed beneath his cushion. He stopped me. I said, "you never save anything from me." He replied,

هذه الصادقة، ما سمعت من رسول الله ﷺ ليس
بينى وبينه أحد. إذا سلمت لى هذه وكتاب الله
والوهط فلا أبالى على ما كانت عليه الدنيا

This is the "Sadiqah" (the Script of Truth). It is what I heard from the Holy Prophet ﷺ. No other narrator intervenes between him and myself. If this script, the Book of Allah and Wahaz (his agricultural land) are secured for me, I would never care about the rest of the world (1).

This Script remained with his children. His grandson, Amr ibn Shuaib used to teach the ahadith contained in it. Yahya ibn Ma'in and Ali ibn al Madini have said that every tradition reported by *Amr ibn Shuaib* in any book of *hadith* has been taken from this script (2). *Ibn al Asir* says that this script contained one thousand ahadith (3).

---

(1). جامع بيان العلم ج ١ ص ٧٢ ، وأسد الغابة ج٣ ص ٢٣٣ و ٢٣٤

(2). تهذيب التهذيب ص ٤٩ و ٥٣ ج٨

(3). أسد الغابة ج٣ ص ٢٣٣

The Script Of Anas

Sayyiduna *Anas ibn Malik* was one of those companions of the Holy Prophet ﷺ who knew writing. His mother had brought him to the Holy Prophet ﷺ when he was ten years old. He remained in the service of the Holy Prophet ﷺ for ten years during which he heard a large number of *ahadith* and wrote them down. *Said ibn Hilal* , one of his pupils says,

كنّا إذا أكثرنا على أنس بن مالك رضى الله عنه فأخرج إلينا مجالّ عنده فقال: هذه سمعتها من النّبى ﷺ فكتبتها وعرضتها

When we insisted upon *Anas* he would bring to us some note-books and say, " These are what I have heard and written from the Holy Prophet ﷺ, after which I have presented them to the Holy Prophet for confirmation (1).

It shows that sayyiduna *Anas* رضي الله عنه had not only written a large number of *ahadith* in several note books, but had also showed them to the Holy Prophet ﷺ who had confirmed them.

The Script Of Ali

It is well known that *Sayyiduna 'Ali* رضي الله عنه had a script of *ahadith* will him. He says,

ما كتبنا عن النبى ﷺ إلاّ القرآن وما فى هذه الصّحيفة

I have not written anything from the Holy Prophet ﷺ except the Holy Quran and what is

(1). مستدرك الحاكم ، ذكر أنس رضي الله عنه ص ٥٧٣ و٥٧٤ ج ٣

contained in this script (1).

Imam *Bukhari* has mentioned this script at six different places of his *Sahih*. A combined study of all those places reveals that this script was substantially large and it consisted of ahadith about Qisas (retaliation), *Diyah* (blood money), Fidyah(ransom), rights of the non-muslim citizens of an Islamic state , some specific kinds of inheritance, *Zakah* rules pertaining to camels of different ages, and some rules about the sanctity of the city of Madinah.

The script was written by Sayyiduna Ali رضي الله عنه in the days of the Holy Prophet ﷺ. Then, in the days of his *khilafah* (rule), he felt that the ahadith of the Holy Prophet ﷺ should be spread among the people to widen the range of Islamic knowledge and to refute certain misguided ideas prevalent in those days.

It is reported by the famous historian *Ibn Sa'd* that he stood in the mosque and delivered a lecture. Then he asked the people,

من يشترى علما بدِرهم

Who will purchase 'knowledge' for one Dirham only?.

He meant that whoever wanted to learn ahadith, should buy writing paper for one dirham and come to him, for dictation of the *ahadith* of the Holy Prophet ﷺ.

It is reported that *Harith al A'war* bought some paper and came to him:

فكتبَ له علما كثيرا

So, Ali wrote for him a lot of knowledge (2)

It should be kept in mind that the word 'knowledge' in the early centuries of Islamic history was used for the knowledge of

---

صحيح البخاري ، كتاب الجهاد ، باب إثم من عاهد ثم غدر ص ٤٥١ ج ١.(1)

طبقات ابن سعد ص ١٦٨ ج ٦ .(2)

ahadith only (1).

Scripts Of Jabir

Jabir ibn Abdullah is one of the famous companions of the Holy Prophet ﷺ who has narrated a large number of ahadith. It is established that he had compiled the *ahadith* in two scripts. One of them contained a detailed account of the last Hajj performed by the Holy Prophet ﷺ. The full text of this script is found in the *Sahih* of *Muslim* wherein he has described even the minute details of the last Hajj (2).

His second script contained other ahadith relating to different subjects.

Qatadah the famous pupil of *Jabir* says:

لأنا لصحيفة جابر أحفظ منّى لسورة البقرة

I remember the script of Jabir more than I remember Surah *Al-Baqarah* of the Holy Quran(3).

Reference to this script is also found in the *Musannaf* of *Abdurrazzaq* where some ahadith of this script are reported (4).

Scripts Of Ibn 'Abbas

Abdullah ibn'Abbas was the cousin of the Holy Prophet ﷺ. When the Holy Prophet ﷺ passed away, he was

---

(1) طبقات ابن سعد ص ٤٦٩ ج ٥ .

(2) صحيح مسلم، كتاب الحج ص ٣٩٤ - ٤٠٠ Zahabi says that this is a replica of Jabir's script (تذكرة الحفاظ للذهبي ١: ٤١)

(3) تهذيب التهذيب ٨ : ٣٥٣

(4) مصنف عبد الرزاق حديث ٢٠٢٧٧ ج ١١ .

yet very young. In order to preserve *ahadith*, he began to compile what he himself heard from the Holy Prophet ﷺ as well as those narrated by other companions. Whenever he came to know of any companion having some *ahadith*, he would travel to him to hear them. All such *ahadith* were compiled by him in several scripts. These scripts numbered so many that they could be loaded on a camel. These scripts remained with his pupil Kuraib. *Musa ibn'Uqbah*, the famous historian says:

وضعَ عندنا كُرَيب حمل بعيرٍ أو عدل بعيرٍ من كتب ابن عبّاس. قال: فكان على بن عبد الله بن عبّاس إذا أراد الكتاب كتبَ إليه: ابعث إلىّ بصحيفة كذا وكذا. قال: فينسخها فيبعث إليه بإحداهما

> *Kuraib* left with us a camel load of *Ibn Abbas*'s books. When *Ali ibn'Abdullah ibn Abbas* would need any book from them, he wrote to *Kuraib*, "Send to me such and such books". He would then transcribe the book and send to him one of the two copies (1).

The pupils of Ibn'Abbas would copy these scripts and read them over to him to confirm the correctness of the copies(2).

Sometimes *Ibn'Abbas* would narrate the *ahadith* to his pupils while they would record them (3).

These are only a few examples of efforts made by the companions of the Holy Prophet ﷺ for the compilation of *ahadith*. We do not intend here to present an exhaustive survey of such efforts. Detailed books can be consulted for this purpose. Our purpose here was to give only some examples. These concrete

---

(1). طبقات ابن سعد ص ٤٩٣ ج ٥

(2). جامع الترمذي ، كتاب العلل ص ٢٦١ ج ١

(3). سنن الدارمي ص ١٠٦ ج ١ حديث ٥١٠ وص ١٠٥ ج ١ حديث ٥٠٥

examples are more than sufficient to refute the fallacious assumption that the *ahadith* were never written in the days of the Holy Prophet ﷺ and his companions.

THE COMPILATION OF AHADITH IN THE ERA AFTER THE COMPANIONS

The history of the compilation of *ahadith* after the companions is even more vast and detailed. Each companion who narrated the *ahadith* had a large number of pupils who compiled what they heard from him. The pupils of the companions are called '*Tabi'in*'.

The compilations of the Tabi'in were generally not arranged subject wise, though some of them have arranged the *ahadith* under subjective headings. The first known book of *hadith* which is so arranged is '*Al-abwab* of Imam *Sha'bi* (b.19 A.H.D.103A.H.). This book was divided into various chapters. Each chapter contained the *ahadith* relating to the same subject like *salah*, *zakah* etc (1).

This proves that the first book of *ahadith* arranged in a regular manner appeared in the very first century. Another book was written by *Hasan Al Basri* (d.110) in which he compiled *ahadith* containing any explanations or commentaries of the Holy Quran (2). This was also a regular book written on a particular subject which appeared in the first century.

In the era of the Tabi'in the compilation of *ahadith* was undertaken officially by the famous khalifah, '*Umar ibn Abdul Aziz* (99-101 A.H.). He issued an official order to all governors

---

(1) تدريب الراوي ص ٤٠ .

(2) السنة قبل التدوين، عجاج الخطيب ص ٣٢٨ .

under his domain that they should gather the knowledgeable persons from among the companions of the Holy Prophet ﷺ and their pupils and write down the *ahadith* found with them (1).

The result of this official decree was that several books of *ahadith* were prepared and spread all over the country. *Ibn Shihab Al Zuhri* was one of the pioneers of the compilation of *hadith* in this period. He has written a number of books.

All these books and scripts written in this period were afterwards included in the larger books of *hadith* written later on, as is usual in the evolution of every science. The separate entity of these books and scripts, being uncalled for, was not much attended to. Thus, the larger books written in the second and third centuries gradually took their place, and being more comprehensive, detailed and sufficient, they were so widely spread and studied that the books of the *Tabi'in* no longer remained on the scene.

However, some manuscripts of these books were preserved. Later books were compared and confirmed by such preserved manuscripts.

One of the books written in the days of the *Tabi'in* was the script of *Hammam ibn Munabbih*, a pupil of *Abu Hurairah* who prepared a book containing *ahadith* he heard from *Abu Huraira* رضي الله عنه .This book is also known as "*Al-Sahifah al Sahihah*". All the ahadith of this book were included in later compilations. The full text of it is also found in the *Musnad* of *Imam Ahmed*. The original script of this book was thus not attended to and was lost for a considerable time.

n 1373 A.H. (i.e. 1954 A.D.) two manuscripts of this book were discovered in the libraries of Berlin and Damascus, and were published by Dr. Muhammad Hamidullah with a detailed

---

(1) . فتح الباري ص ١٧٤ ج ١

introduction.

Dr. Muhammad Hamidullah edited these manuscripts which were written centuries ago. He has als compared their text with the one narrated in the *musnad* of Imam Ahmed. He could not find any material differnce between the two texts. There are few very minor differences of negligible words which always exist between two manuscripts of the same book.

It proves that the books of the *Tabi'in* were included and were thus made part of the later books of hadith, with all necessary precautions by which they can safely be relied upon.

THE COMPILATIONS OF THE FIRST CENTURY

We present here a list of hadith works written by the Tabi'in in the first and second centuries. In the first century the following books of *hadith* were compiled by the Tabi'in (A).

1. Book of *Khalid ibn Ma'dan* (d.104)

2. Books of *Abu Qilabah* (d.104). He *bequeathed* his books to his pupil, *Ayyub Saktiyani* (68-131 A.H.), who paid more than ten Dirhams as a fare for them being loaded on a camel.

3. The script of *Hammam ibn Munabbih*, already referred to.

4. Books of *Hasan al Basri* (21-110 A.H.)

(A) For reference see the following:-

(1) تذكرة الحفاظ للذهبي ١ : ٨٨ و ١ : ١٦٦ .

(2) طبقات ابن سعد ٥ : ٢١٦ وتذكرة الحفاظ ١ : ٨٨ .

(3) صحيفة همام بن منبه بتحقيق الدكتور حميد الله .

(4) طبقات ابن سعد ٧ : ١٧ والمحدث الفاصل .

5. Books of *Muhammad al Baqir* (56-114 A.H.)

6. Books of *Makhul from Syria*

7. Book of *Hakam ibn 'Utaibah*

8. Book of *Bukair ibn 'Abdullah ibn al Ashajj* (d.117)

9. Book of *Qais ibn Sa'd* (d.117). This book later belonged to *Hammad ibn Salamah*

10. Book of *Salaiman al Yashkuri*

11. *Al Abwab of Sha'bi, already* referred to.

12. Books of *Ibn Shihab al Zuhri.*

13. Book of *Abul-'Aliyah*

14. Book of *Said ibn Jubair* (d.95 A.H.)

15. Books of *Umar ibn Abdullah Aziz* -(61-101 A.H.)

16. Books of *Mujahid ibn Jabr* (d 103 A.H.)

17. Book of *Raja ibn Hywah* (d.112 A.H.)

---

(5) تهذيب التهذيب ٢ : ١٠٤ .

(6) الفهرست لابن النديم ص ٣١٨ .

(7) تقدمة الجرح والتعديل ص ١٣٠ .

(8) تهذيب التهذيب ١٠ : ٧٠ و ٧١ .

(9) تذكرة الحفاظ ١ : ١٩٠ .

(10) تقدمة الجرح والتعديل ص ١٤٤ و ١٤٥ .

(11) تدريب الراوي ص ٤٠ .

(12) جامع بيان العلم ١ : ١٧٦ .

(13) السنة قبل التدوين (تعليق) ص ٣٣٨ .

(14) تقييد العلم ص ١٠٢ .

(15) سنن الدارمي ١ : ١٢٩ وتقييد العلم ص ١٠٨ .

(16) تاريخ بغداد للخطيب ١١ : ٢٣٢ .

(17) سنن الدارمي ١ : ١٢٩ وتقييد العلم ص ١٠٨ .

18. Book of *Abu Bakr ibn Muhammad ibn Amr ibn Haq*

19. Book of *Bashir ibn Nahik.*

THE BOOKS OF HADITH WRITTEN IN THE SECOND CENTURY

The basic characteristic of the books written in the second century is that a large number of them were arranged subject wise, while the books of the first century were not. However, compilations without due arrangement contined in this century too. The list of books compiled in this period is very long. Few prominent books are referred to here (B).

1. Book of *Abdulmalik ibn Juraij* (d.150 A.H.)

2. *Muwatta, of Malik ibn Anas* (93-179 A.H.)

3. *Muwatta, of Ibn Abi Zi'b* (80-158 A.H.)

4. *Maghazi of Muhammad ibn Ishaq* (d.151 A.H.)

5. *Musnad of Rabi' ibn Sabih* (d.160 A.H.)

6. Book of *Sa'id ibn Abi 'Arubah* (d.156 A.H.)

7. Book of *Hammad ibn Salmah* (d.167 A.H.)

8. *Jame' Sufyan al Thauri* (97-161 A.H.)

9. *Jame' Ma'mar ibn Rashid* (95-153 A.H.)

10. Book of *Abdurrahman al Awza'i* (88-157 A.H.)

---

(18) تقدمة الجرح والتعديل ص ٢١ .

(19) طبقات ابن سعد ٧ : ١٦٢ .

(B) For no.1 to 14 see:

المحدث الفاصل ص ١٥٥ وتدريب الراوي ص ٤٠ ومقدمة فتح الباري ص ٤

الرسالة المستطرفة :and for the remainder see والسنة قبل التدوين ص ٣٣٧

11. *Kitab al zuhd* by *Abdullah ibn al Mubarak* (118-181)

12. Book of *Hushaim ibn Bashir* (104-183 A.H.)

13. Book of *Jarir ibn Abdulhamid* (110-188 A.H.)

14. Book of *Abdullah ibn Wahb* (125-197 A.H.)

15. Book of *Yahya ibn Abi Kathir* (d.129 A.H.)

16. Book of *Muhammad ibn Suqah* (d.135 A.H.)

17. *Tafsir of Zaid ibn Aslam* (d.136 A.H.)

18. Book of *Musa ibn 'Uqbah* (d.141 A..H)

19. Book of *Ash'ath ibn 'Abdulmalik* (d.142)

20. Book of *Aqil ibn Kahalid* (d.142 A.H.)

21. Book of *Yahya ibn Sa'id Ansari* (d.143)

22. Book of *Awf ibn Abi Jamilah* (d.146)

23. Books of *Jafar ibn Muhammad al Sadiq* (d.148)

24. Book of *Yunus ibn Yazid* (d.152 A.H.)

25. Books of *Abdurrahman almas'udi* (d.160)

26. Books of *Zaidah ibn Qudamah* (d.161)

27. Books of *Ibrahim al Tahman* (d.163)

28. Books of *Abu Hamzah al Sukri* (d.167)

29. *Algharaib by Shu'bah ibn al hajjaj* (d.160)

30. Books of *'Abdul Aziz ibn 'Abdullah al Majishun* (d.164 A.H.)

31. Books of *Abdullah ibn Abdullah ibn Abi Uwais* (d.169)

32. Books of *Sulaiman ibn Bilal* (d.172)

33. Books of *'Abdullah ibn Lahi'ah* (d.147)

34. *Jame' Sufyan ibn 'Uyainah* (d.198)

35. *Kitabul-Athar by Imam Abu Hanifah* (d.150)

36. *Maghazi of Mu'tamir ibn Sulaiman* (d.187)

37. *Musannaf of Waki 'ibn Jarrah* (d.196 A.H.)

38. *Musannaf of Abdurrazzak ibn Hammam* (136-221)

39. *Musnad of Zaid ibn 'Ali* (76-122)

40. Books of *Imam Shafi'i* (15-204)

The following books written in this age are still available in printed forms.

1. *Almuwatta*, by *Imam Malik.*

2. *Kitabul - Athar* by *Imam Abu Hanifah.*

3. *Musannaf* by *'Abdurrazzaq.*

This book has been published in eleven big volumes.

4. *As - sirah* by *Muhammad ibn Ishaq.*

5. *Kitab - al - Zuhd* by *'Abdullah ibn al - Mubarak.*

6. *Kitab - al - Zuhd* by *Waki 'ibn Jarrah* (3 volumes).

7. *Almusnad* by *Zaid ibn 'Ali* (76 - 122).

8. *Sunan* of *Shafi'i* (150 - 204).

9. *Musnad* of *Shafi'i.*

10. *Siyar* of *Awza'i* (88 - 157).

11. *Musnad* of *'Abdullah ibn al Mubarak* (d. 181).

12. *Musnad of Abu Dawood Tayalisi* (d. 204).

13. *Al - Radd 'Ala Siyaril - Awza'i by Imam Abu Yusuf.*

14. *Al - Hujjah 'ala Ahlil Madinah* by *Imam Muhammad ibn Hasan Shaibani*.

15. *Kitabul - Umm by Imam Shafi'i.*

16. *Al - Maghazi by Waqidi* (130 - 206) (4 volumes).

This list is by no means exhaustive. But a careful study of these books only which are available today in printed forms, would clearly reveal that their style is much developed and they definitely do not seem to be the first books on their subject. Some of them are in more than ten volumes, and their arrangement shows that the compilation of *hadith* in those days reached a developed stage.

All these valuable efforts of compiling the *ahadith* belong to the first and second centuries. Hence, one can easily see how false is the assumption that the compilation of ahadith did not take place before the third century.

What we have cited above is more than sufficient to prove that the compilation of ahadith has begun in the very days of the Holy Prophet ﷺ and has continued in each point of time thereafter. This process has, no doubt, passed through certain stages as is usual in every new science or branch of knowledge. But the assumption that the process could not begin before the third century cannot be substantiated on any ground whatsoever.

THE CRITICISM OF AHADITH

Although the task of preserving of *ahadith* through all the four ways mentioned earlier including compilations in written form, has been performed with due diligence throughout the first four centuries of Islamic history, yet it does not mean that all the traditions narrated or compiled in this period have been held as true and reliable.

In fact, in the same period in which the work of the compilation of *ahadith* was going on, a very systematic scienec of criticism was developed by the scholars of *hadith* in which numerous tests were suggested to verify the correctness of a narration. All these tests were applied to each and every tradition or report before holding it reliable. The different branches of knowledge which have been introduced by the scholars of the science of *hadith* has no parallel in the art of historical criticism throughout world history. It is not possible for us to herein present even a brief introduction of these different branches and the valuable works produced in this respect. It may be said without any fear of exaggeration that thousands of books have been written on these different branches of knowledge regarding the science of *hadith*.

It will be pertinent, however, to give a brief example of the nature of the criticism of *ahadith* carried on by scholars and the different tests applied by them to ascertain the veracity of a *hadith*.

The traditions viewed from different angles have been classified into hundreds of kinds. Relative to their standards of authenticity, the traditions are ultimately classified into four major categories:

(a) *Sahih* (correct)

(b) *Hasan* (good enough)

(c) *Da'if* (weak)

(d) *Maudu'* (coined)

Only the first two kinds are held to be reliable. Precepts of the Shari'ah can be based on and inferred from only these two kinds. Hence, only the ahadith of these two categories are held to be the source of Islamic law. The other two kinds have little or no value especially in the legal or doctrinal matters.

Before declaring a *hadith* as *Sahih* or *Hasan*, the following tests are applied:

(a) Scrutiny of its narrators.

(b) Scrutiny of the constancy of the chain of narrators.

(c) Comparison of its chain and text with other available ways of narration in the same matter.

(d) Examination of the chain and the text of the hadith in the light of other material available on the subject, and to ensure that there is no defect in the chain or in the text.

We will try to give a brief explanation of these four tests as they are applied by the scholars of hadith to scrutinize the veracity of a tradition.

1. Scrutiny of the narrators

The first and foremost test of the correctness of a *hadith* relates to the credibility of its narrators. This scrutiny is carried out on two scores: firstly, examination of the integrity and honesty of a narrator, and secondly, examination of his memory power.

To carry out this scrutiny, a separate complete Science has been introduced which is called *'Ilmur-Rijal* (The knowledge of men). The scholars of this science devoted their lives for the thorough enquiry about each person who has reported a *hadith*. For this, they used to go to his place and enquire about him from his neighbours, pupils and friends so that no scholar would be impressed by his personal relations with a narrator. 'Ali ibn al-Madini, the famous scholar of *Rijal* when asked about his father, first tried to avoid the question and replied "Ask some other scholar about him". But when the question was repeated with a request for his own opinion, he said,

هُو الدِّين ، إنّه ضعيف

> It is the matter of Faith, (I, therefore, reply). He is a weak narrator.

Waki' ibn Jarrah, the well-known Imam of *hadith* held his father as "weak" in hadith, and did not rely on his reports unless they are confirmed by some reliable narrator.

Imam Abu Dawood, the author of one of the Six Books, has opined about his son (1) 'Abdullah, that he was "a great liar".

Zaid ibn Abi Unaisah has said about his brother Yahyah, "Do not accept the traditions of my brother Yahyah, because he is reputed in lying". (2)

Similar opinions are recorded in the books of the '*ilmur-rijal*. Hundreds of books have been written on this subject. Here are only a few examples:

1. *Tahzibuttahzib* by *Hafiz Ibn Hajar*:

Printed in twelve volumes, this book has been designed to give a brief account of all the narrators whose narration is found in the famous Six Books of *hadith* only. It contains the life accounts of 12455 narrators (3), arranged in alphabetical order.

---

(1) This is the same 'Abdullah whose work "Kitabul Masalif" has been published by some orientalists.

(2) الإعلان بالتوبيخ لمن ذم التاريخ ، للسخاوي ص ٦٦ .

(3) This is the total of the members given in each volume separately. Sometimes, the same narrator has been mentioned in different places with different names. So, the actual number of the narrators may be less, but not less than 10,000.

You can pick up any name from any chain of any hadith in any book from the Six Books. This name will certainly be found in the T*ahzibuttahzib* recorded in its place in alphabetical scheme. There you can find his dates of birth and death, the list of his teachers, the list of his pupils, important events of his life and the opinions of the scholars about his credibility.

There are several other books meant for the narrators of the Six Books exclusively, and after consulting them one can easily reach a definite conclusion about the veracity of a narrator.

2. *Lisanul-Mizan by Hafiz Ibn Hajar*

This book is meant exclusively for those narrators whose names do not appear in any chain contained in any of the Six Books. It means that the traditions reported by them are found only in some books other than the Six Books.

This book consists of seven volumes and embodies the introduction of 5991 narrators.

3. Ta'jilul-Manfa'ah by Hafiz Ibn Hajar.

This book is confined to the introductions of the narrators whose traditions are found in the books of the four Imams: Malik, Abu Hanifah, Shafi'i and Ahmed ibn Hanbal, and are not among the narrators of the Six Books. Thus, it contains the introduction of 1732 narrators.

All these three books are written and compiled by the same person, namely, the *Hafiz Ibn Hajar*. It means that he has compiled the introduction of more than seventeen thousand narrators of the hadith.

This is the effort of only a single scholar. Many other

books are available on the same subject. The following table will show the large number of narrators introduced in few famous books of *rijal* which are frequently referred to.

	Name of the book	Author	Volumes	Number of narrators
1.	Al-tarikh al Kabir	Imam Bukhari	9	13781
2.	Al- Jarh wat-ta'dil	Ibn Abi Hatim	9	18050
3.	Tahzibuttahzib	Hafiz Ibn Hajar	12	12455
4.	Mizanul i'tidal	Zahabi	4	11053
5.	Lisanul mizan	Hafiz Ibn Hajar	7	
6.	As-siqat	'Ijli	1	2116
7.	Almughni fid du'afa	Zahabi	2	7854

The last book of this table has introduced only those narrators who have been held as "weak" narrators. Similar books are written by Ibn Abi Hatim, Darqutni etc. On the contrary,there are books which deal with the reliable narrators only like "Thiqat of Ibn Hibban" in eleven volumes.

Anyhow, if a narrator is found to be dishonest, has very weak memory or he is unknown, no trust is placed on his narrations. A large number of traditions has been repudiated on this score alone.

2. Constancy of the chain of narrators

It is well-known that no report, in the science of *hadith* is accepted unless it gives the full chain of narrators upto the Holy Prophet ﷺ, Each narrator from this chain is first scrutinized on the touch-stone of his credibility as dicussed above. But even if all the narrators of a chain are found to be reliable, it is not enough to hold the tradition as authentic. It must be proved that the chain is constant and no narrator has been missed in between. If it is found that some narrator has been missed at any stage, the tradition is held to be unreliable. To ensure the constancy of the chain, it is necessary to know about each narrator whether it is possible for him historically to meet the person from whom he claims to hear the tradition.

This scrutiny is indeed very difficult and delicate. But the scholars of the science of *hadith* have undertaken this task in such an accurate manner that one cannot but wonder.

While holding an enquiry about each narrator, the scholars, beside ascertaining his integrity and memory, would also survey his teachers and pupils. Thus, a detailed list of both his teachers and pupils is available in each detailed book of *Rijal*. So, when deciding about the constancy of a *hadith* the scholars do not only make themselves sure about the dates of birth and death of each narrator, but also examine the list of his teachers and pupils.

Not only this, they often try to fix the time-span in which a narrator had opportunities to meet a particular teacher and that in which he did actually hear *ahadith* from him. On the basis of this information they derive certain important conclusions about the credibility of a narrator.

For example, *'Abdullah ibn Lahi'ah* is a well-known Egyptian narrator of hadith. It is established that his memory was weak and he used to narrate those traditions which he wrote. At a particular time, his house was burnt by fire and all his books were also burnt. After this occurance he sometimes used to report *ahadith* from his memory. Therefore, some scholars have decided that his narrations before the accident are reliable while those narrated after it are not worthy of trust. Now, the pupils who have heard *ahadith* from him in the early period, their narrations may be accepted, while the reports of those who have heard from him in the later period cannot be relied upon. The scholars have scrutinised the list of his pupils and have specified the names of his early pupils like *'Abdullah ibn Wahb* etc. and have declared that all the rest should be treated as his later pupils, and no trust might be placed on their narrations.

In short, the second type of scrutiny, which is very essential in the criticism of traditions, relates to the constancy and perpetuity of the chain of narrators. If it is found that a narrator has not heard the hadith directly from the one to whom he is ascribing it, the tradition is said to be *Munqati'* (broken) which cannot be treated as reliable.

3. Comparison with other narrations

The third test applied to a tradition relates to its comparison with what is narrated by other pupils of the same teacher.

Sometimes a tradition is repoted by several narrators. All these reports about the same saying or event are said to be the "*turuq*" (different ways) of that tradition. While scrutinizing a tradition, the scholars undertake a combined study of all its "ways". If it is found that the majority of the reliable reporters narrate the *hadith* in a particular way, but one of them reports it in a version substantially different from that of the others, his report is held to be a "*Shadh*" (rare) version. In such case, despite the reliability of the reporter, his version is not accepted as a "Sahih" (correct) one, and no trust is placed on it unless it is confirmed and supported by any internal or external evidence.

4. General analysis of the tradition

The last, and very important, scrutiny is accompanied by the general analysis of a tradition. In this scrutiny the tradition is analysed in the light of other relevant material available on the subject. The tradition is examined from different angles: whether the reported saying or event is at all possible; whether the reported. event conforms to the established historical events; whether it's text can be held as truly attributed to the Holy Prophet ﷺ ; whether the chain of narrators is genuine etc.

This is a very dificult and delicate scrutiny which cannot be undertaken successfully unless the scholar has full command over all the relevant subjects,.occupies complete knowledge of *hadith* and has a great skill in the science of criticism of *hadith.*

If, after this scrutiny, a strong doubt appears to a scholar about the authenticity of a *hadith,* he points out that there is a "defect" (*'illah*) in the chain or in the text of the *hadith*, and a tradition having this kind of 'illah' or 'defect' is not held as 'Sahih'.

Thus, a '*Sahih*" (correct) *hadith* has been defined by the scholars as follows:

"What is reported, by a reporter who is honest and of good memory power, without any break in the chain of narrators, without any '*shudhudh*' (rareness) and without any '*illah*' (defect)".

Conclusion

It is not possible for us to give all the details of the critical sciences developed by the scholars of *hadith*. What we have stated in this chapter is only a simple example of the works undertaken by them. It can, however, help one to imagine the altitude of their academic and scientific efforts and to satisfy oneself that the task of 'preservation of *hadith*' has been performed by this ummah with such diligence, precaution and sense of responsibility that one cannot find its parallel in the history of any other community. It was through these efforts that the divine promise of the preservation of the Holy Quran, with all its letters and meanings, was duly fulfilled.